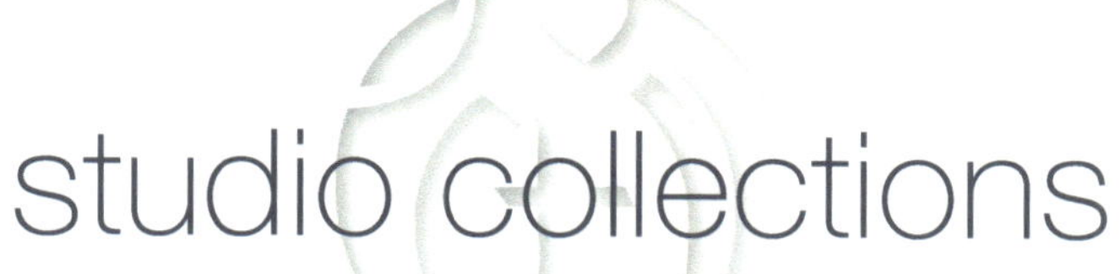

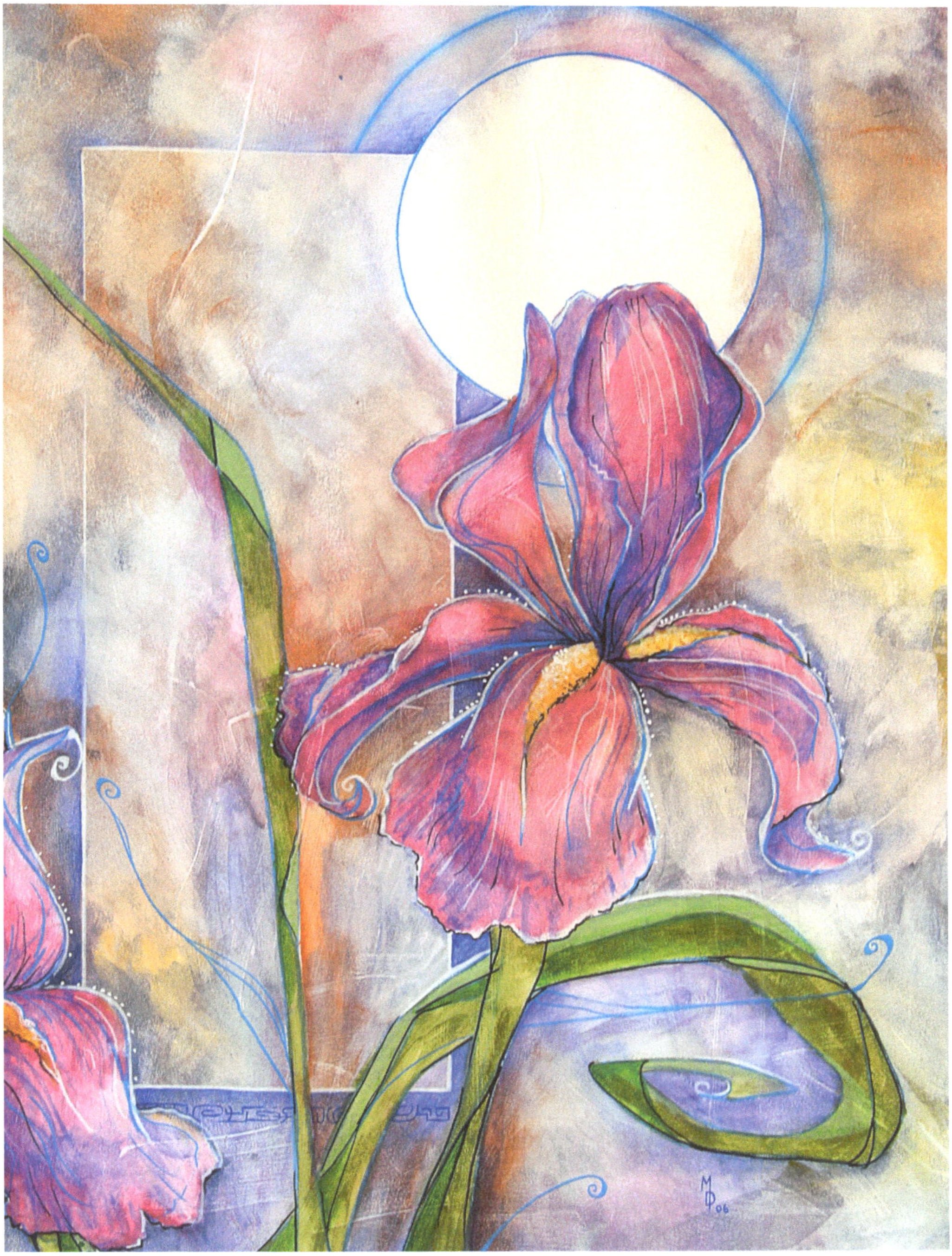

Art by Miles Davis | Funky Florals

Studio Collections | Art by Miles Davis - Funky Florals

Massive Burn Studios
www.massiveburn.com

First Edition 2024

ISBN 979-8-9918816-2-3

Artwork by Miles Davis
Cover Design and Typeset by Merissa Corbet Davis

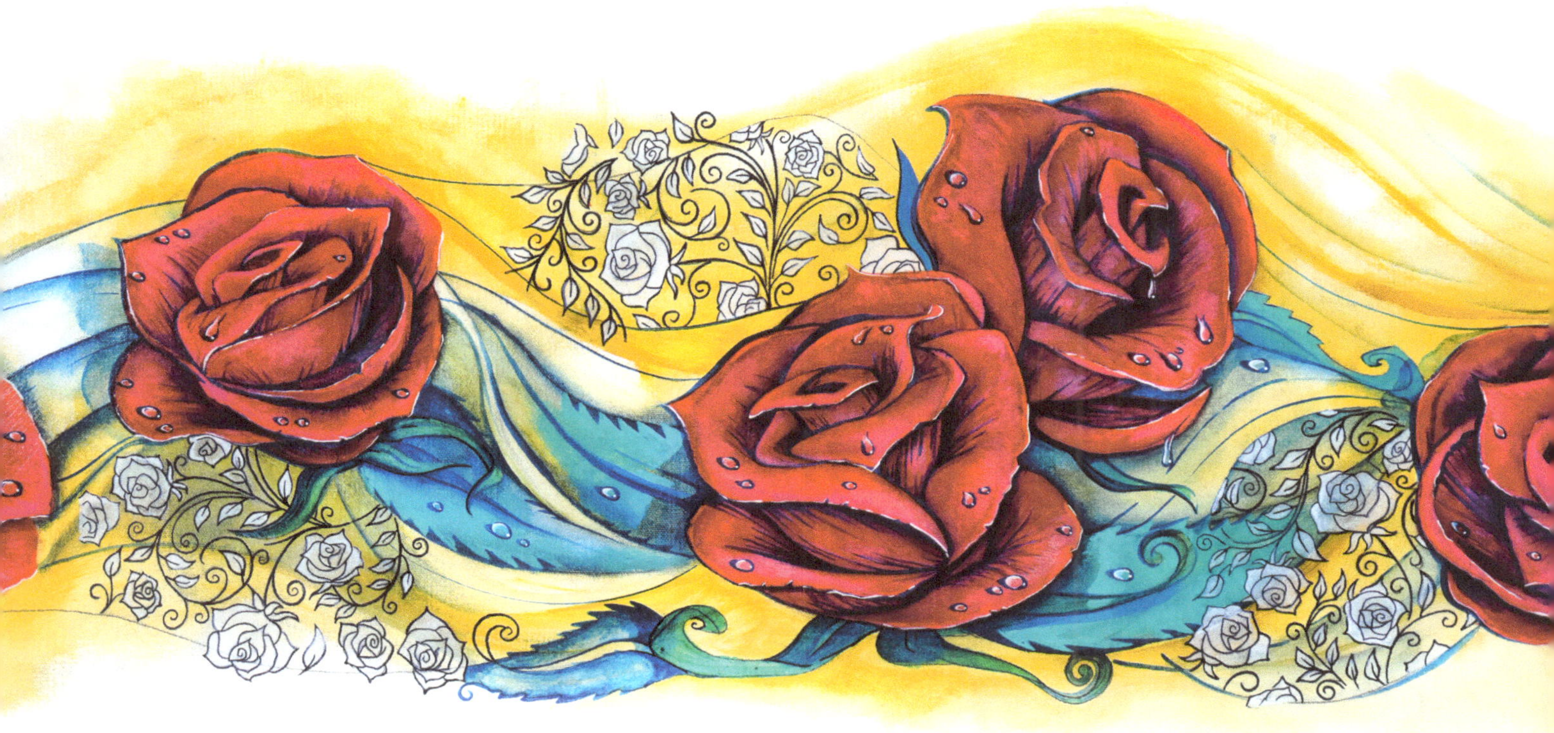

Funky Florals

Discover a series of funky florals by Miles Davis - paintings in which Miles can explore and meld impressionistic characteristics along with his own modern aesthetic. A divergence from his more common figurative work, in this series, Miles draws attention to the whimsical nature of flowers, casting them in a playful light, often cartooning them or pulling in anthropomorphic qualities to distinguish his flowers from the everyday.

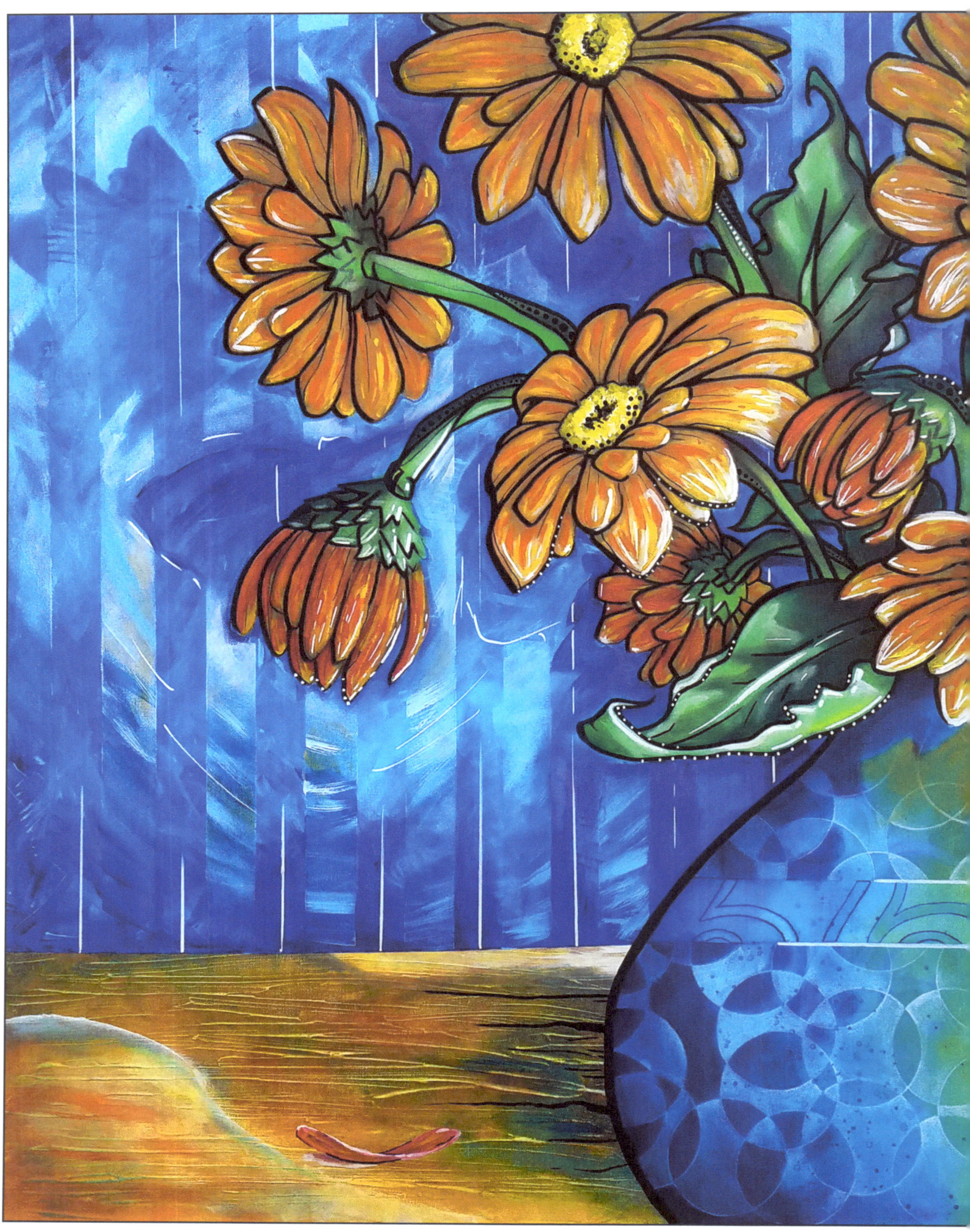

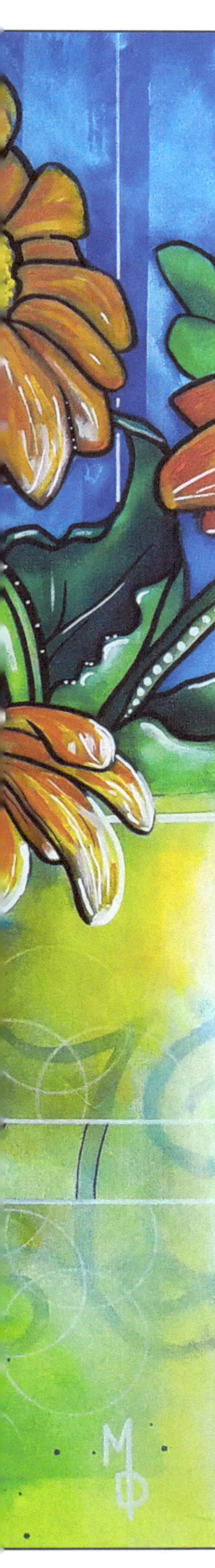

Summertime Gerbers, 2018
36"x36"
Acrylic & Mixed Media on Canvas

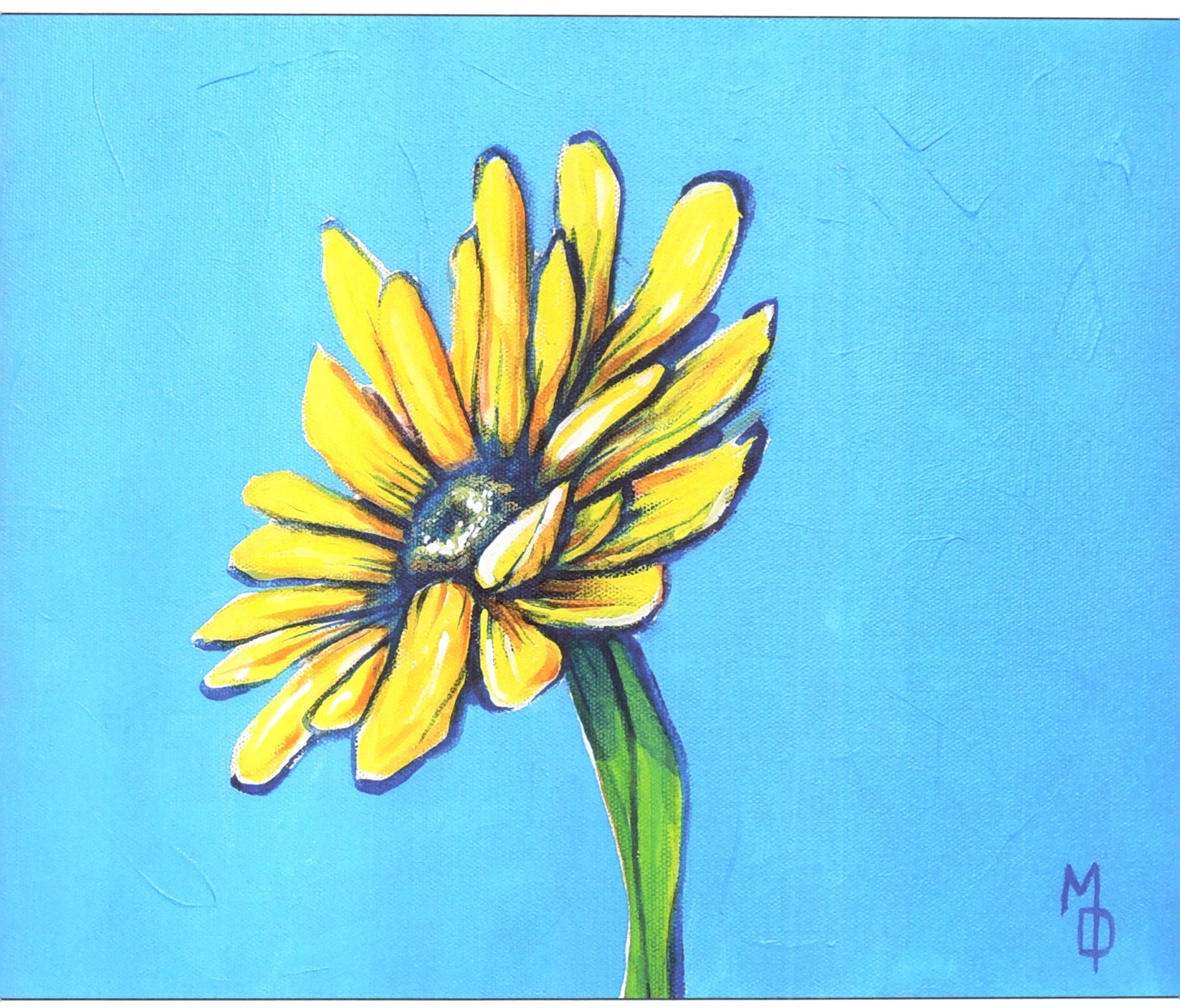

Sunny D, 2020
24"x12"
Acrylic & Mixed Media on Canvas

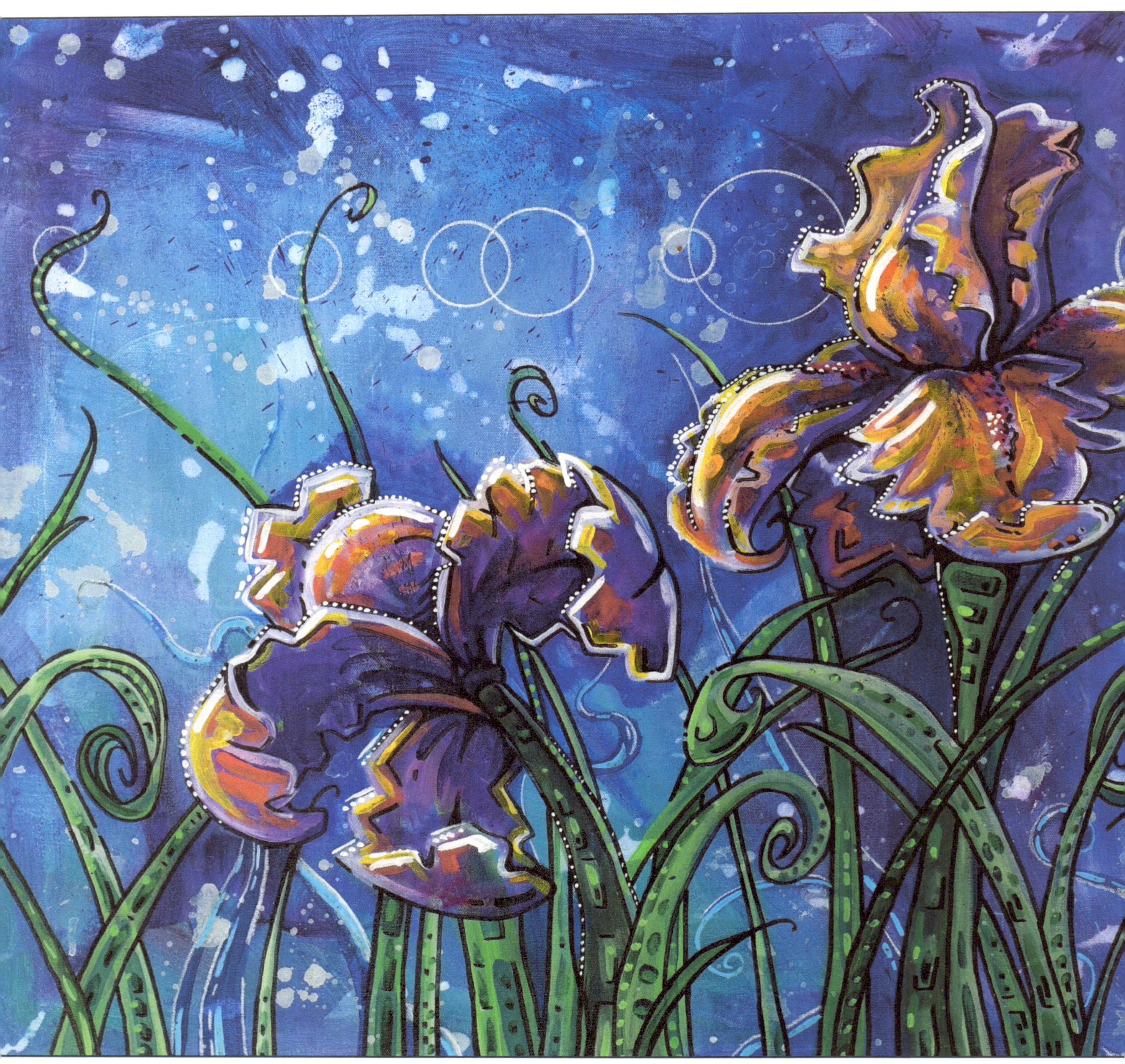

Flowers for Alexia, 2005
48"x24"
Acrylic & Mixed Media on Canvas

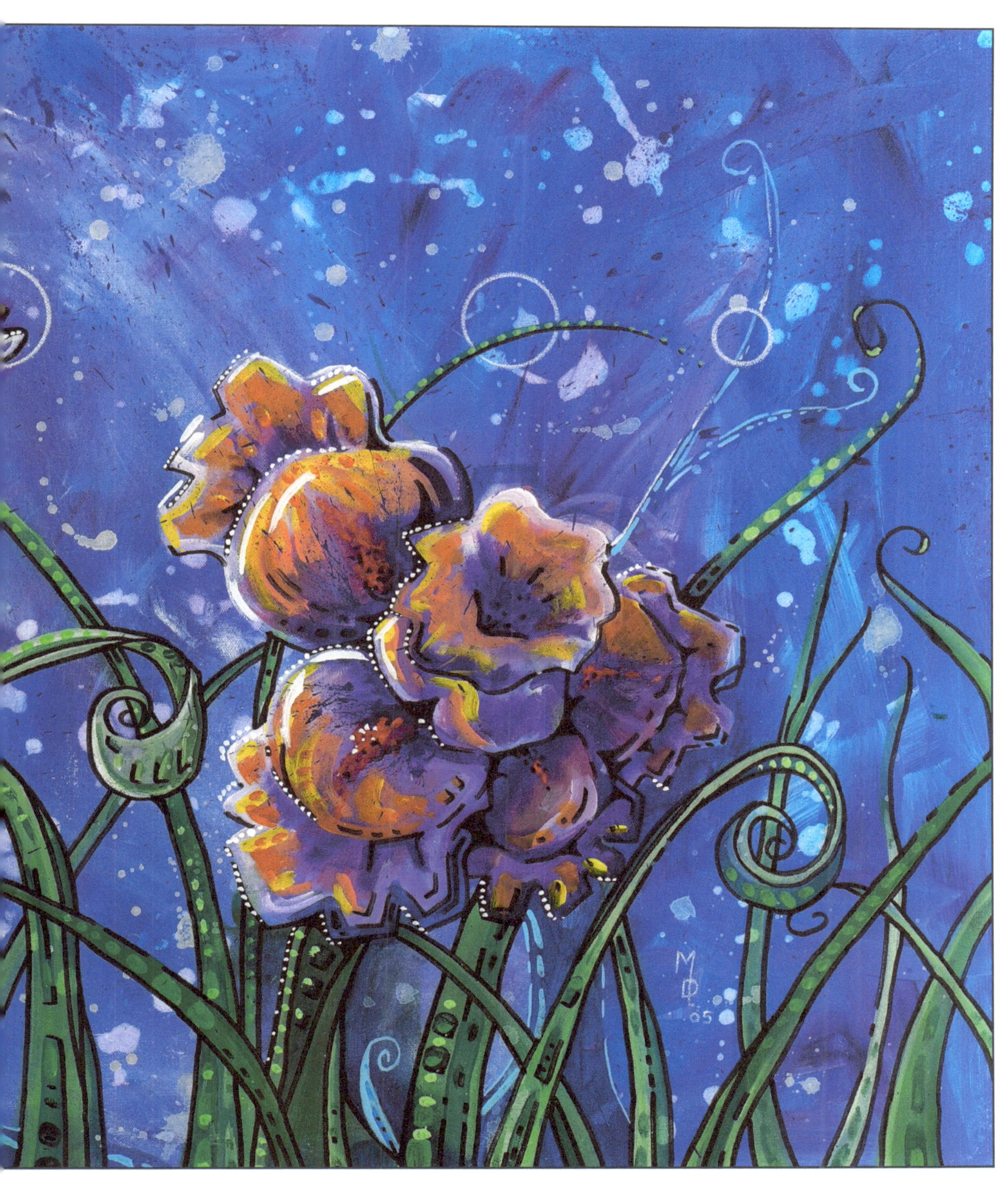

“The faces and anthropomorphic qualities to some of my paintings started as an exploration into the feelings associated with flowers – happiness, cheer, beauty, joy, grief, etc.”

Afternoon Glow, 2022
18"x24"
Acrylic & Mixed Media on Canvas

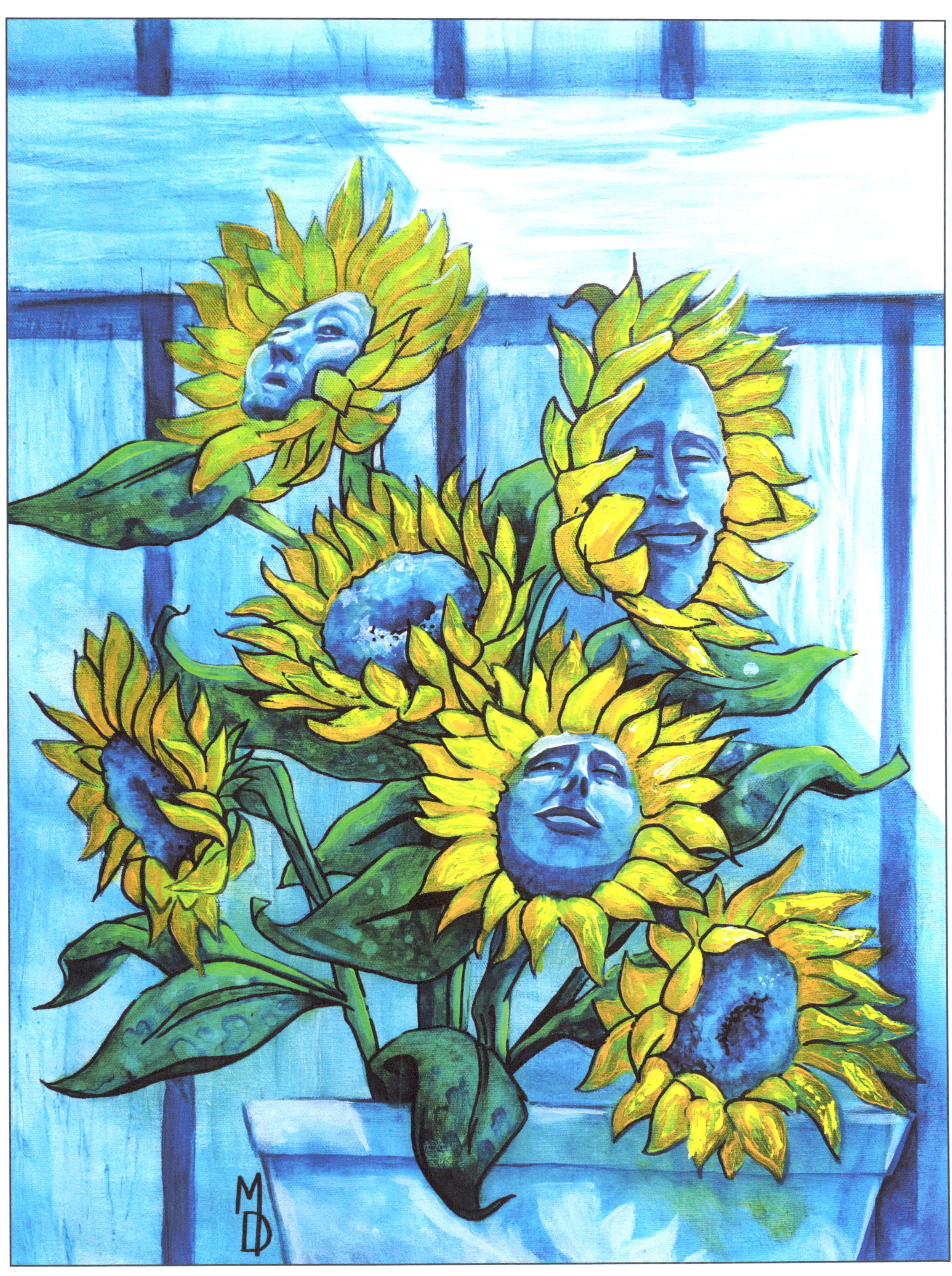

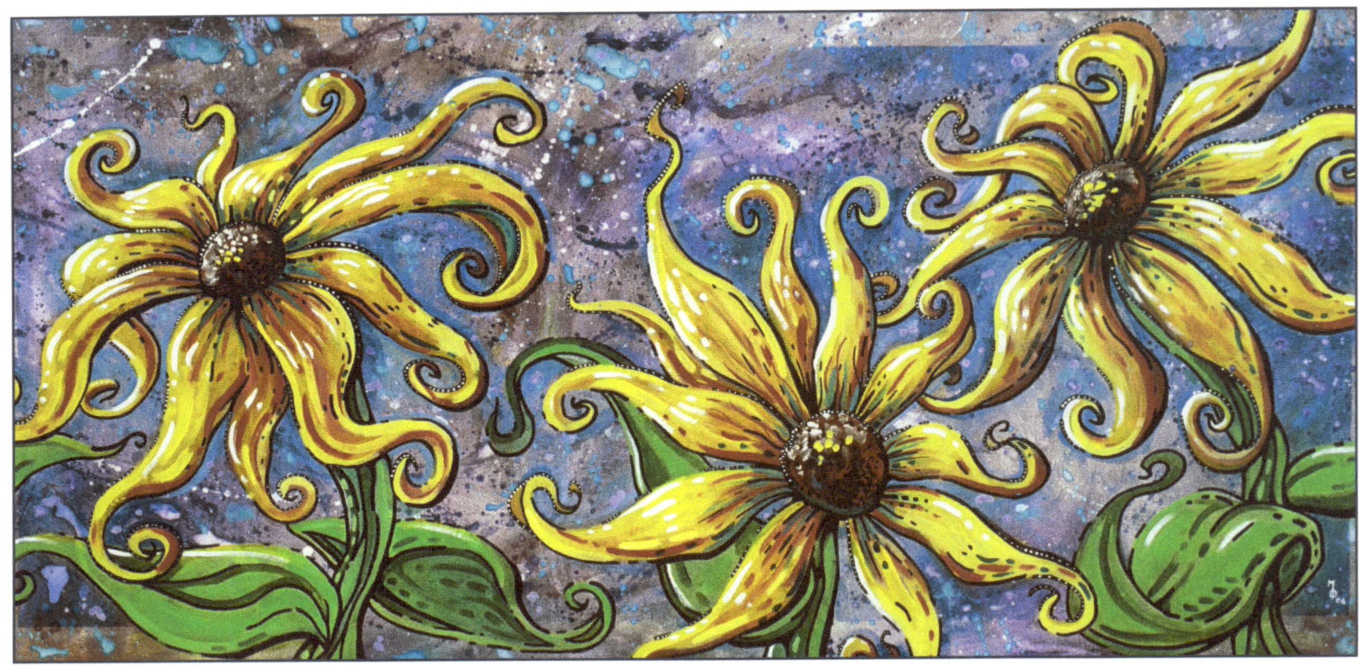

Susans at Dusk, 2006
48"x24"
Acrylic & Mixed Media on Canvas

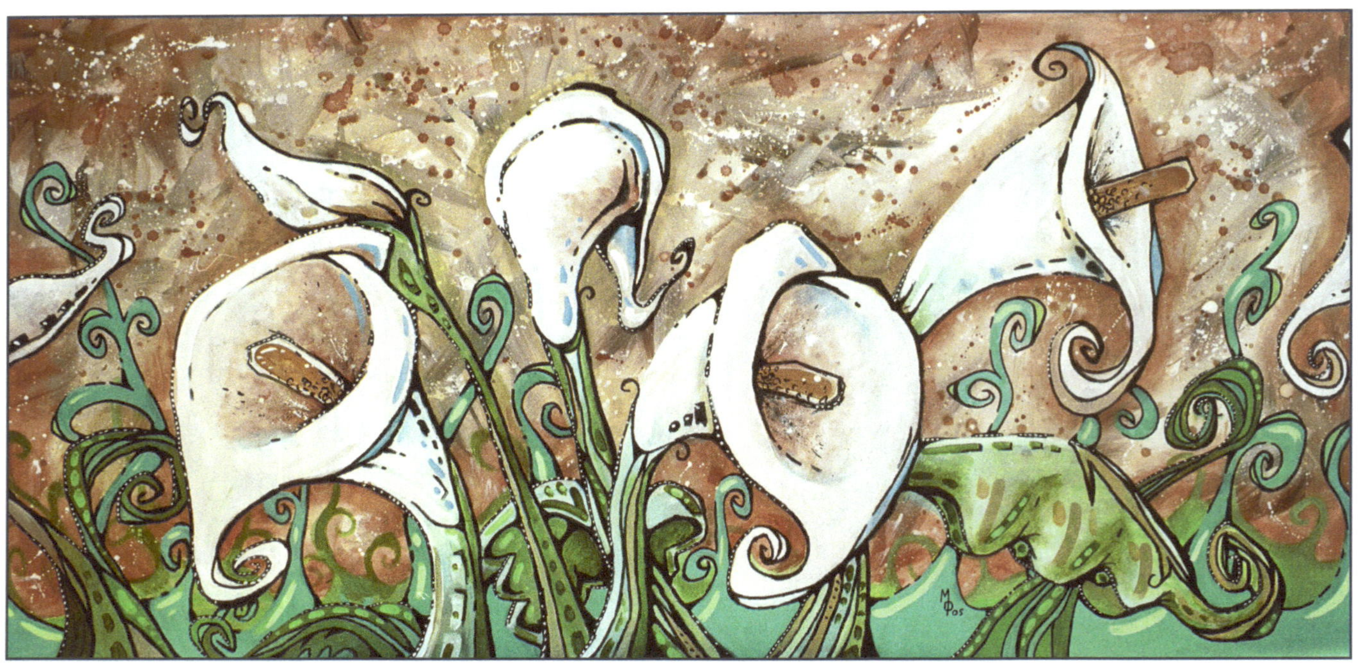

Pasture of Calla Lilies, 2006
48"x24"
Acrylic & Mixed Media on Canvas

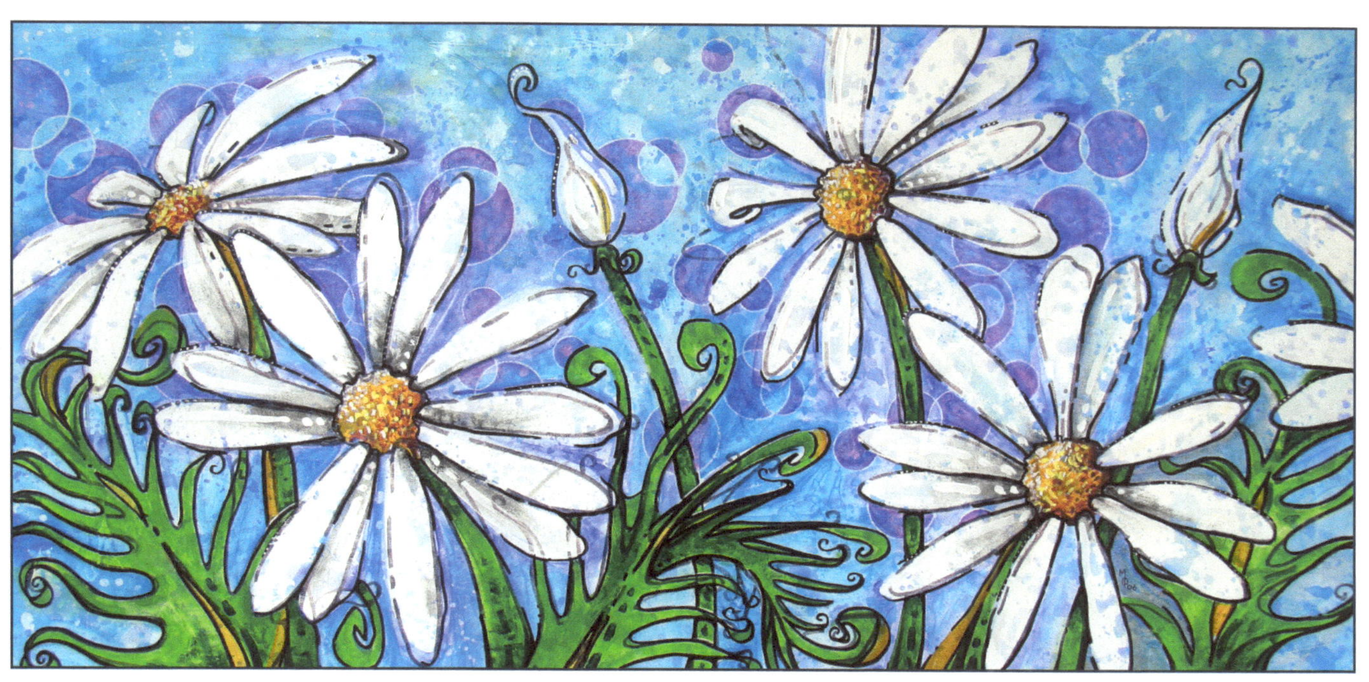

Underwater Daisies, 2006
48"x24"
Acrylic & Mixed Media on Canvas

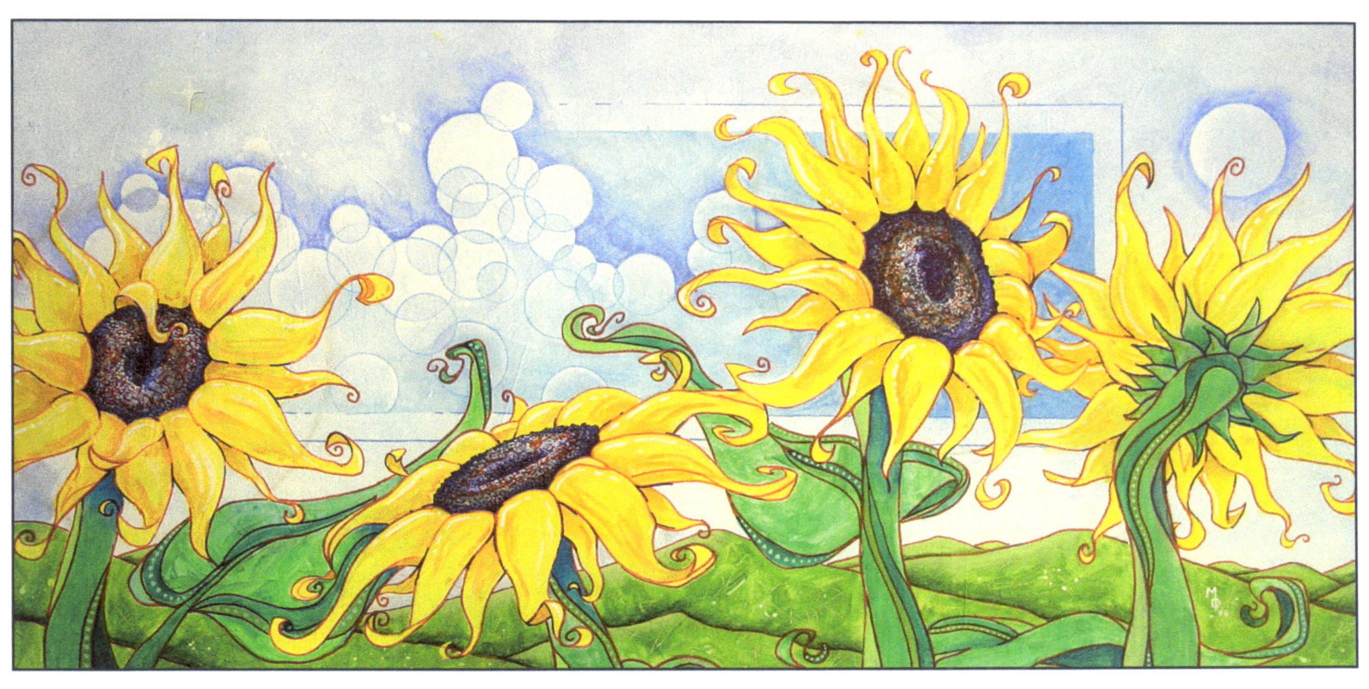

Rolling Hills & Sunflowers, 2006
48"x24"
Acrylic & Mixed Media on Canvas

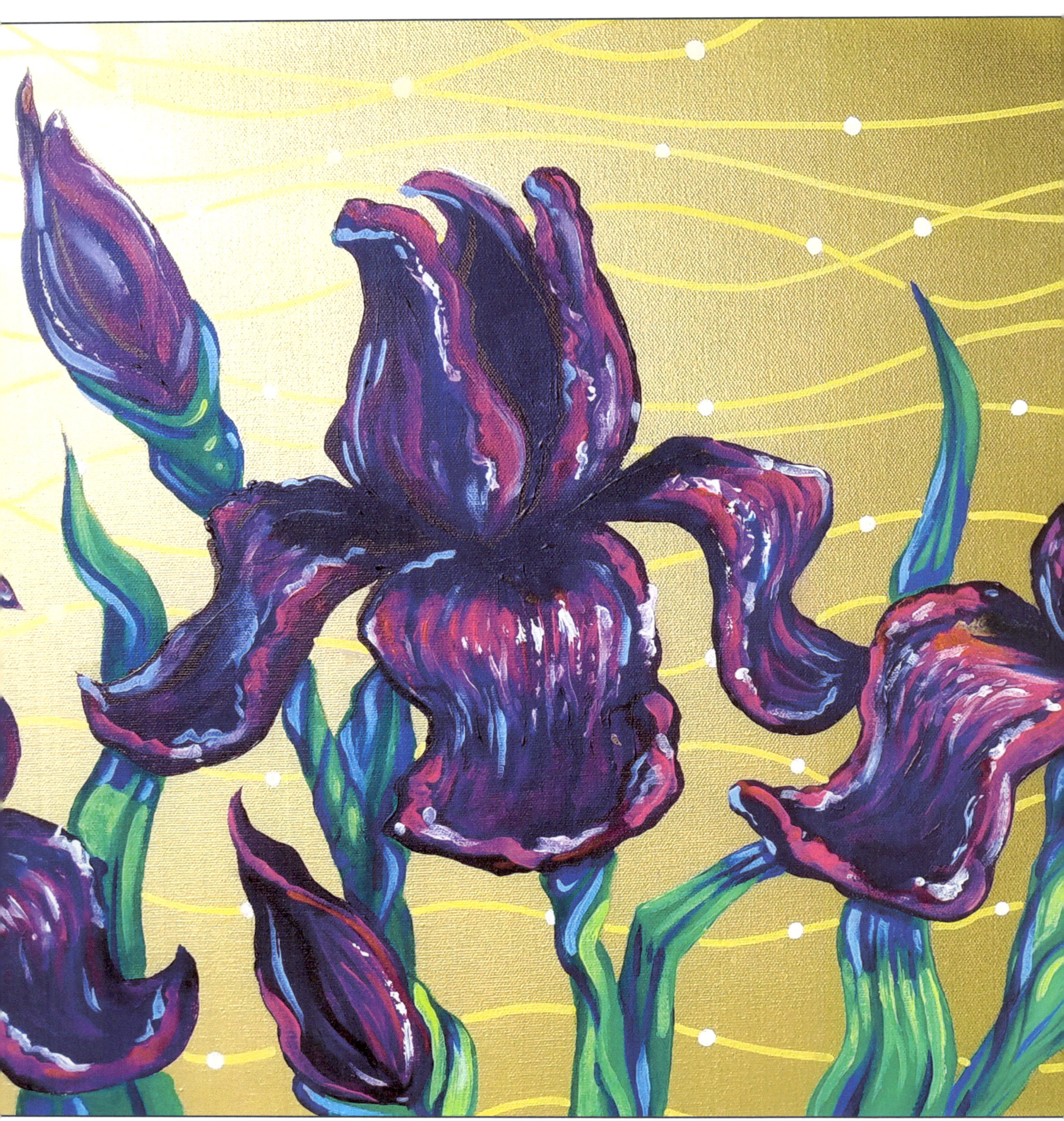

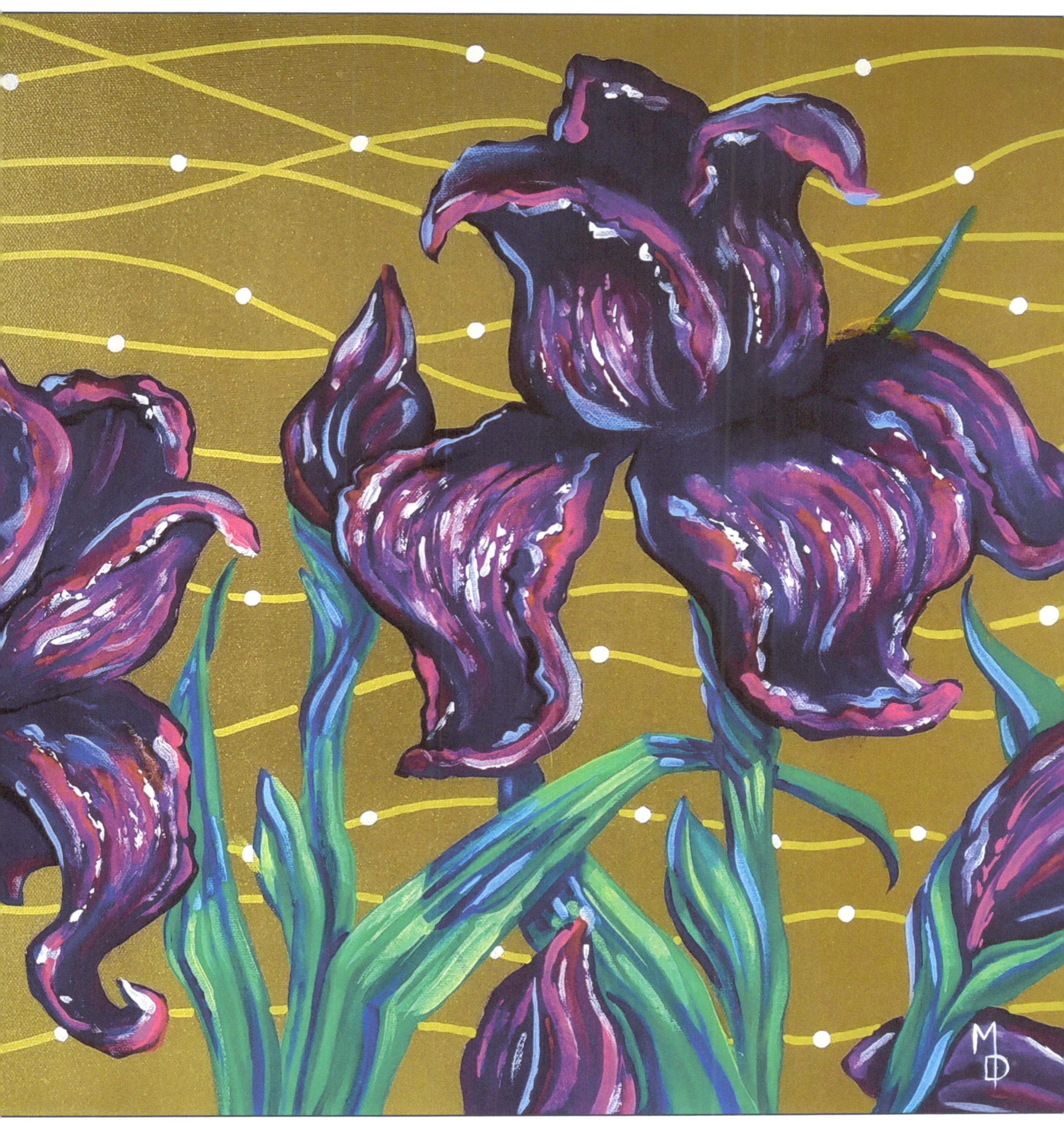

Royal Irises, 2020
36"x18"
Acrylic & Mixed Media, Metallic on Canvas

“Occasionally, I’ll paint the idea of ‘happy.’ This is one of those paintings, and I wanted to make it cartoony to add some whimsy, just play around, and be a little bit goofy.”

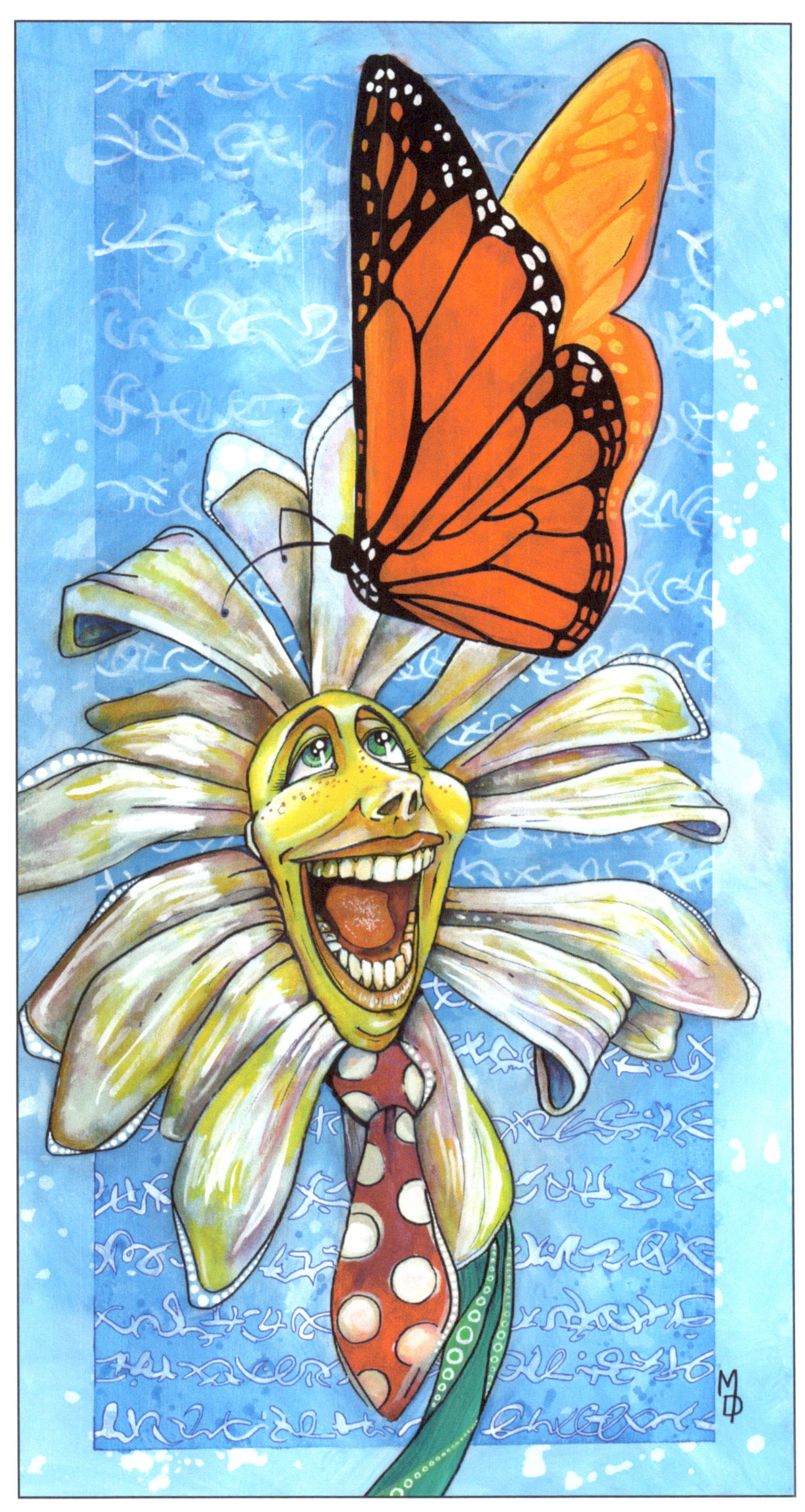

Happy Daisy, 2014
18"x36"
Acrylic & Mixed Media on Canvas

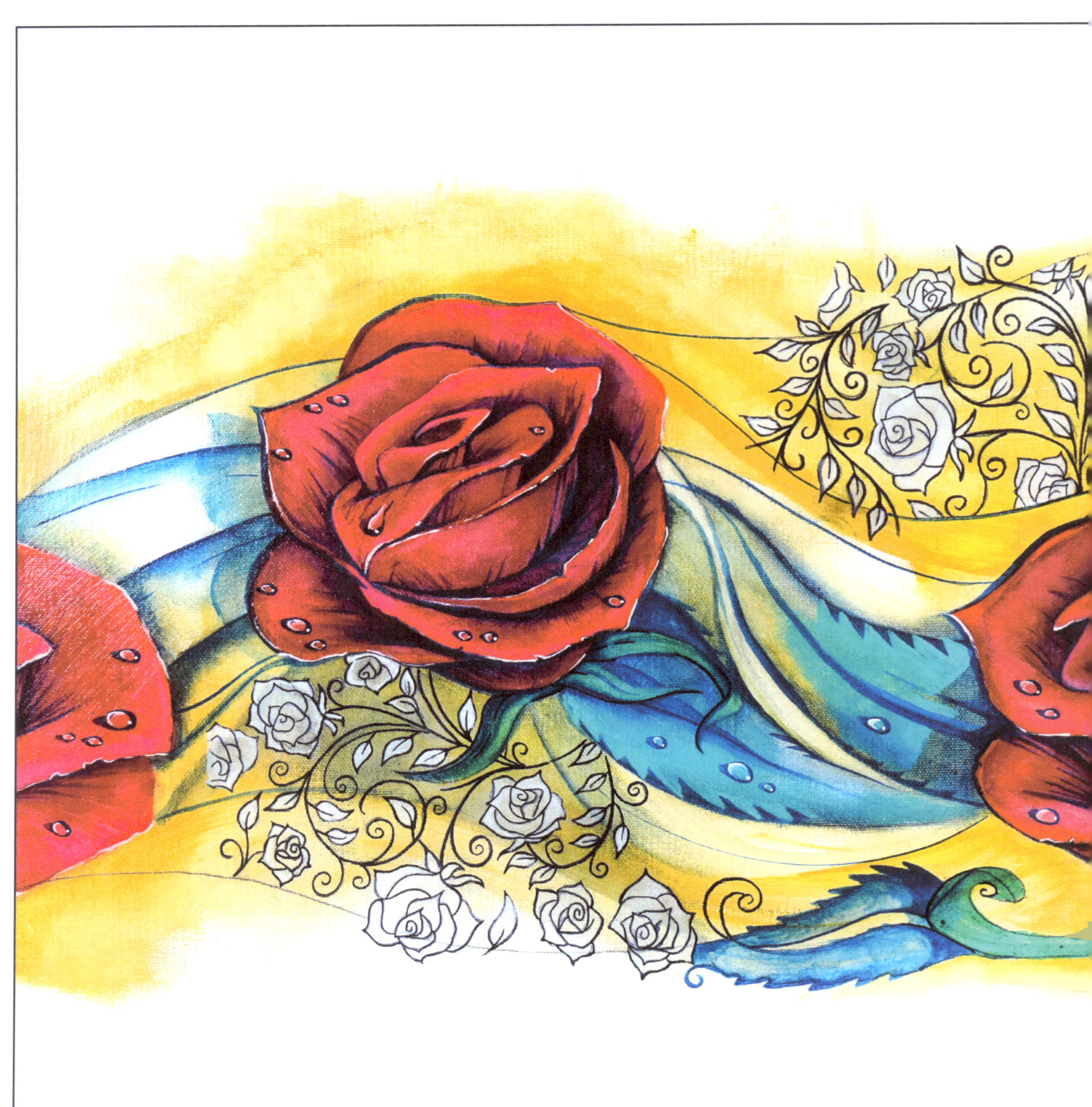

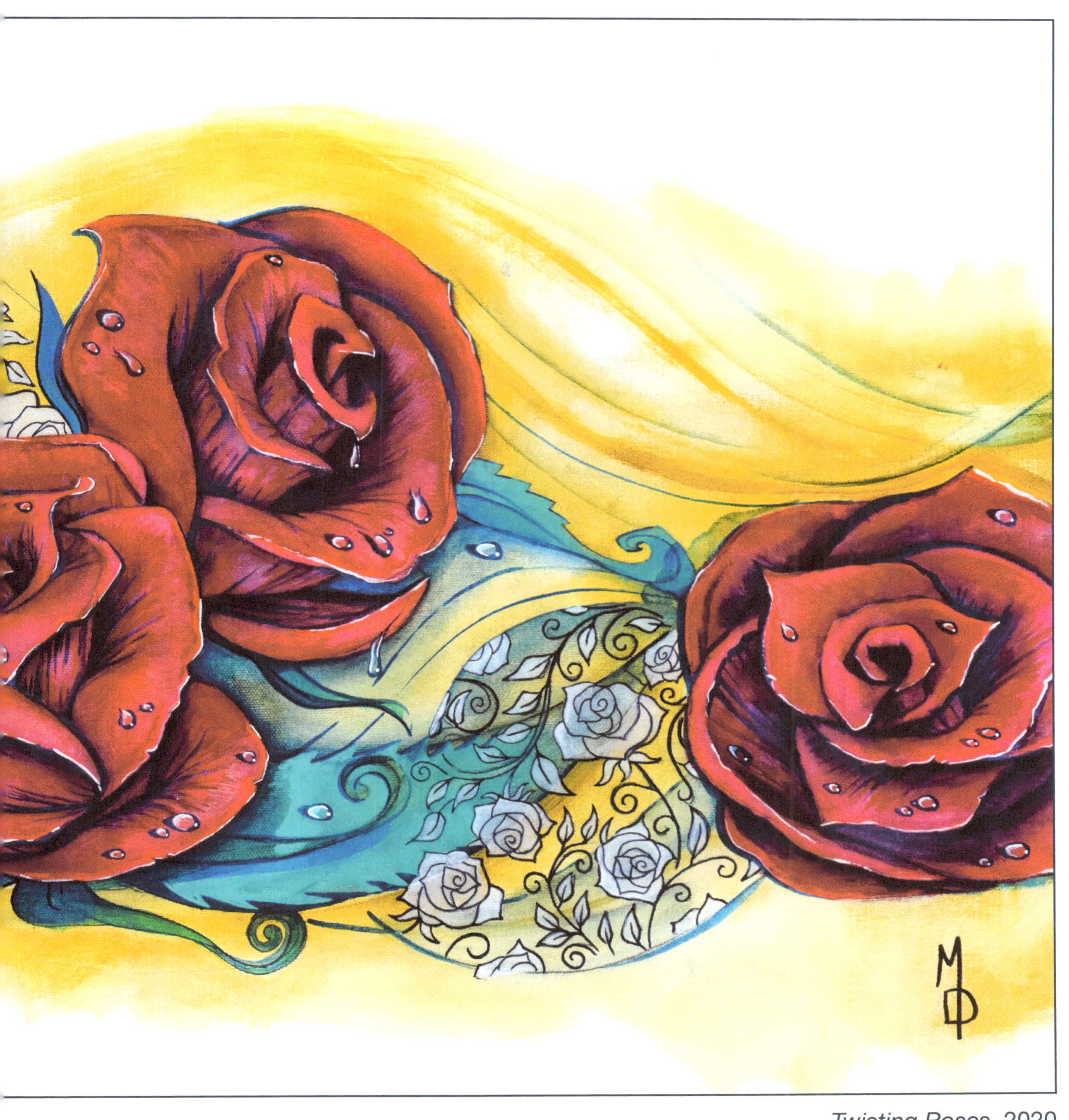

Twisting Roses, 2020
36"x18"
Acrylic & Mixed Media on Canvas

Iris in Twilight, 2006
21"x29"
Acrylic & Mixed Media on Paper

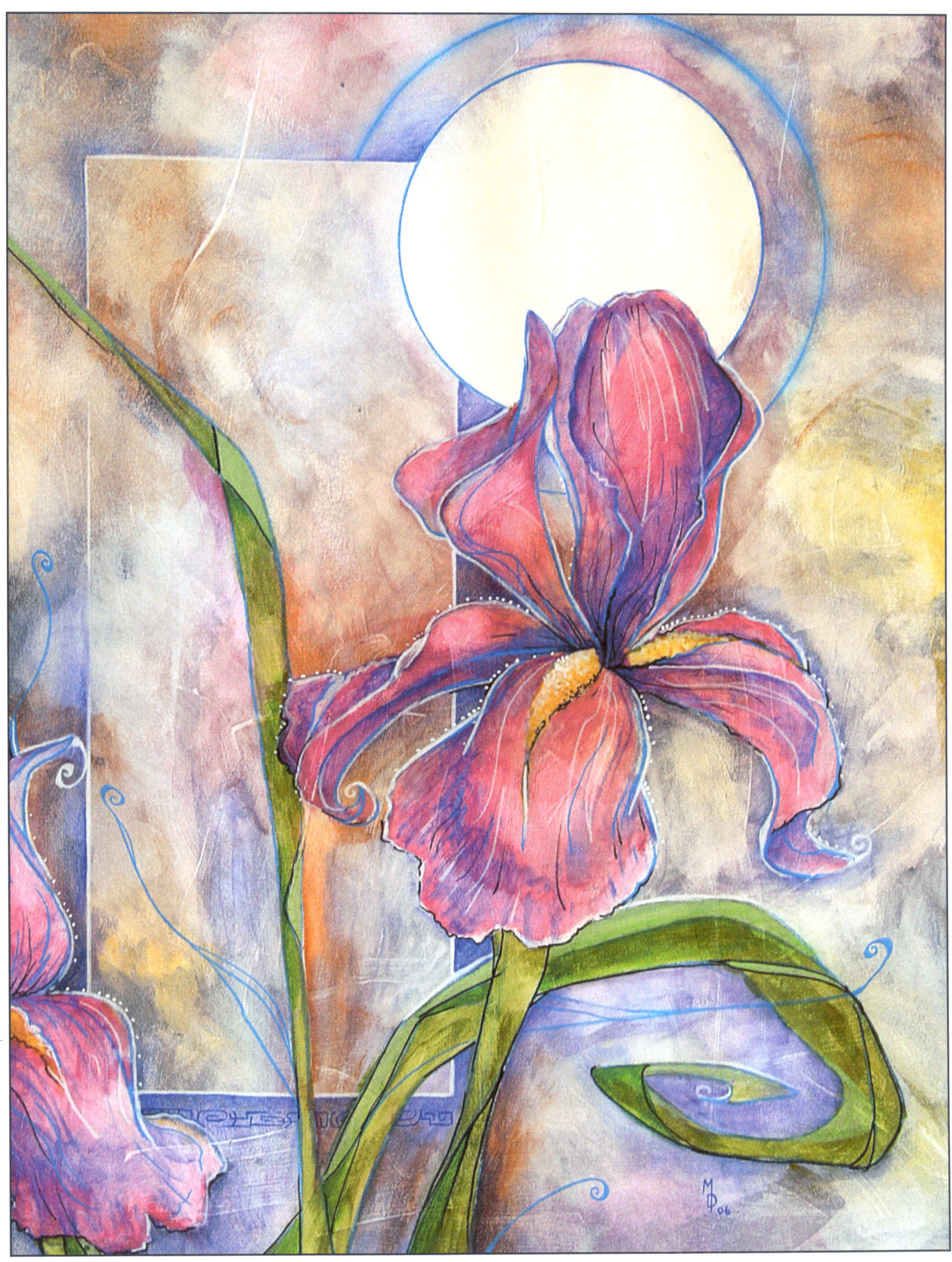

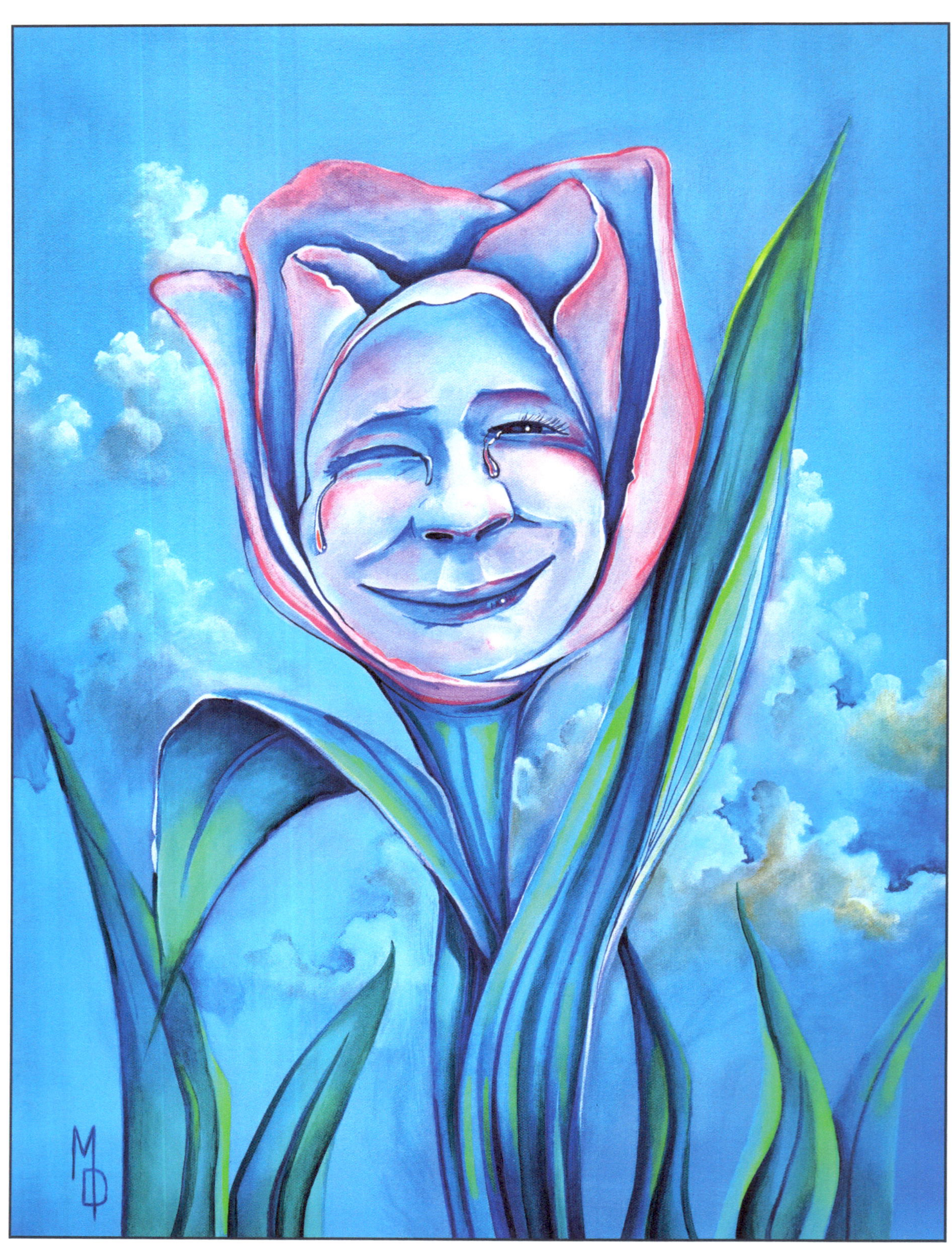

Happy Tears Tulip, 2024
18"x24"
Acrylic & Mixed Media on Canvas
Blacklight Enhanced

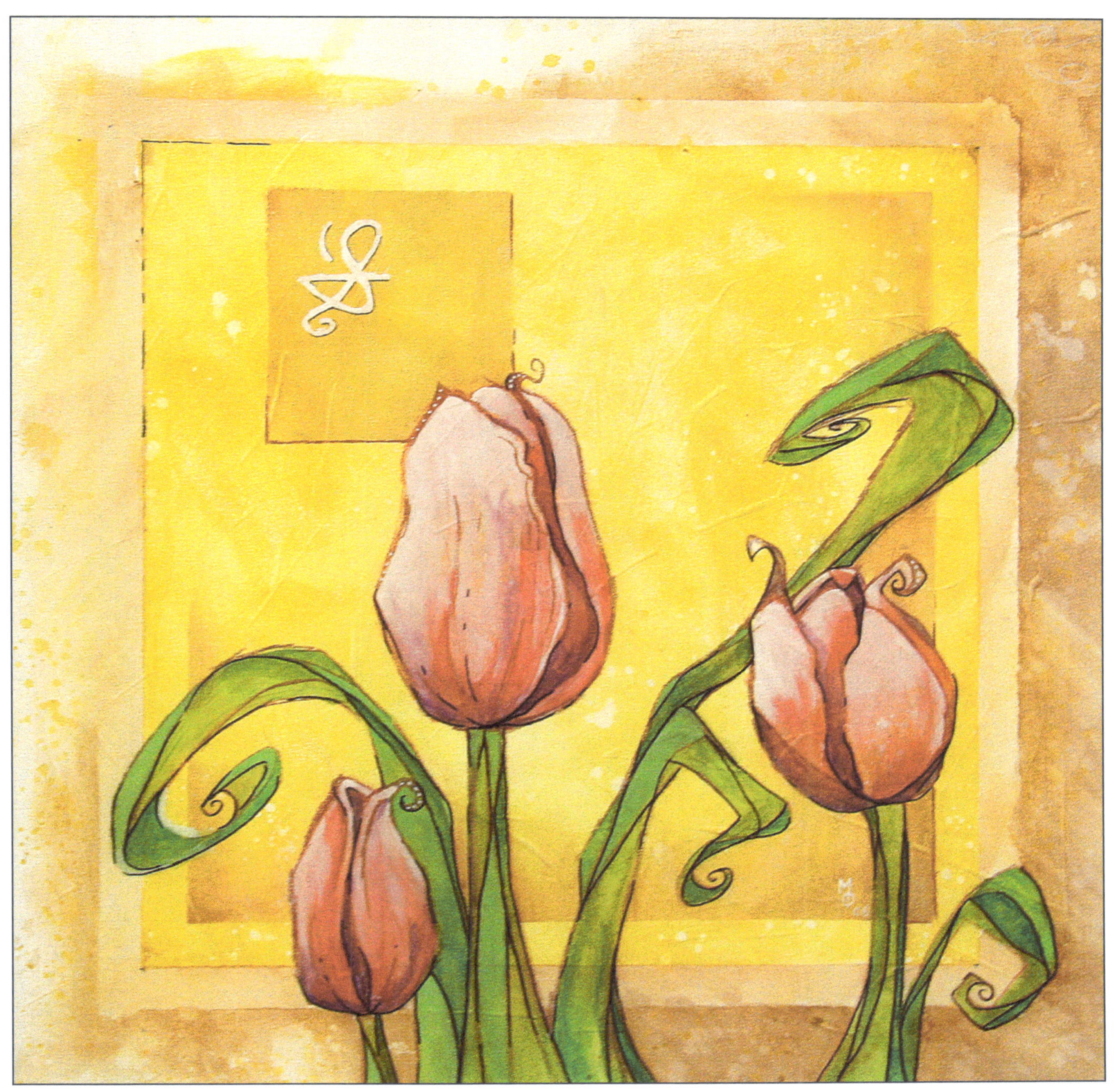

Tulips Squared, 2006
24"x24"
Acrylic & Mixed Media on Canvas

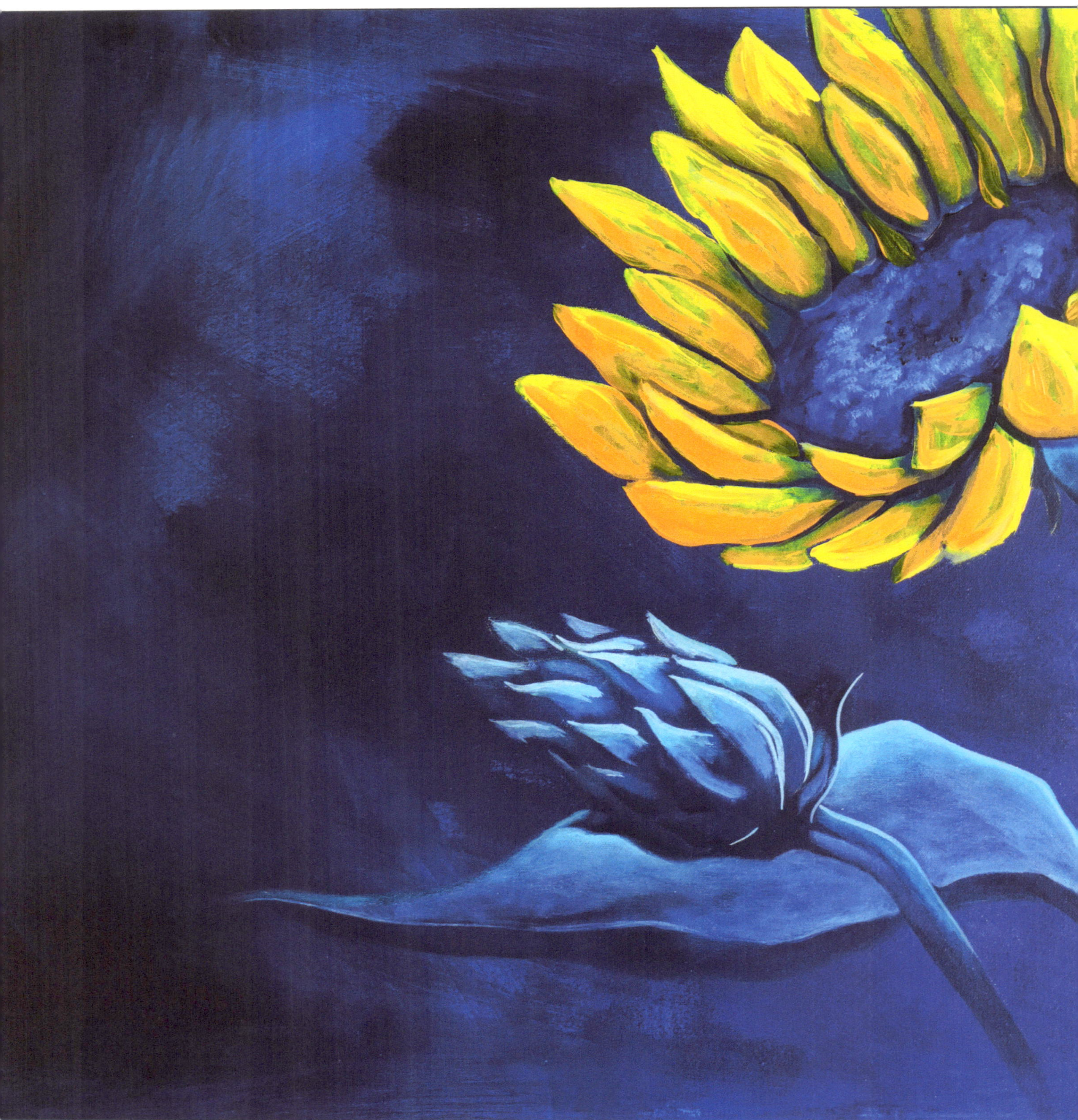

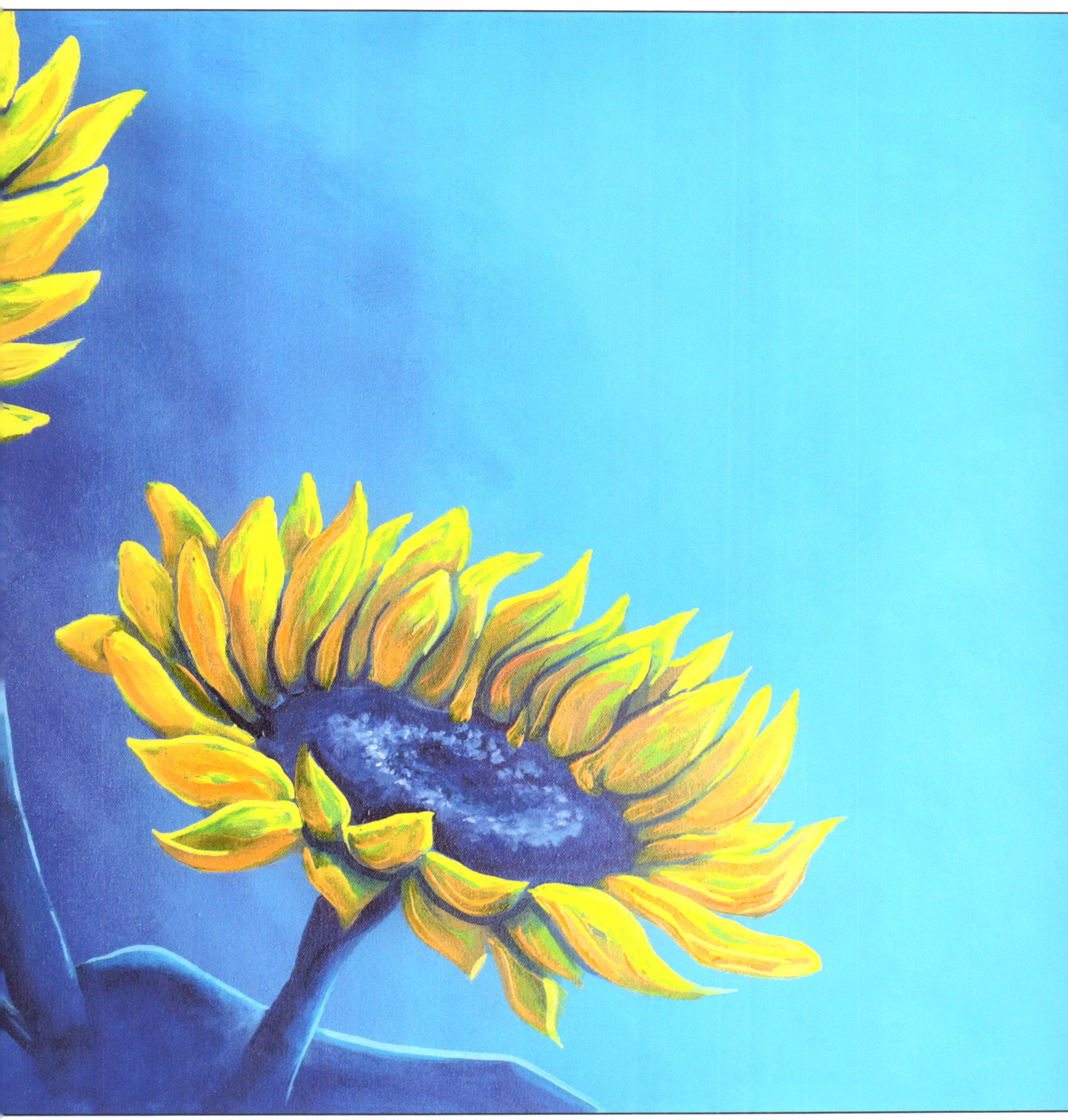

Corbet Sunflowers, 2023
48"x24"
Acrylic & Mixed Media on Canvas

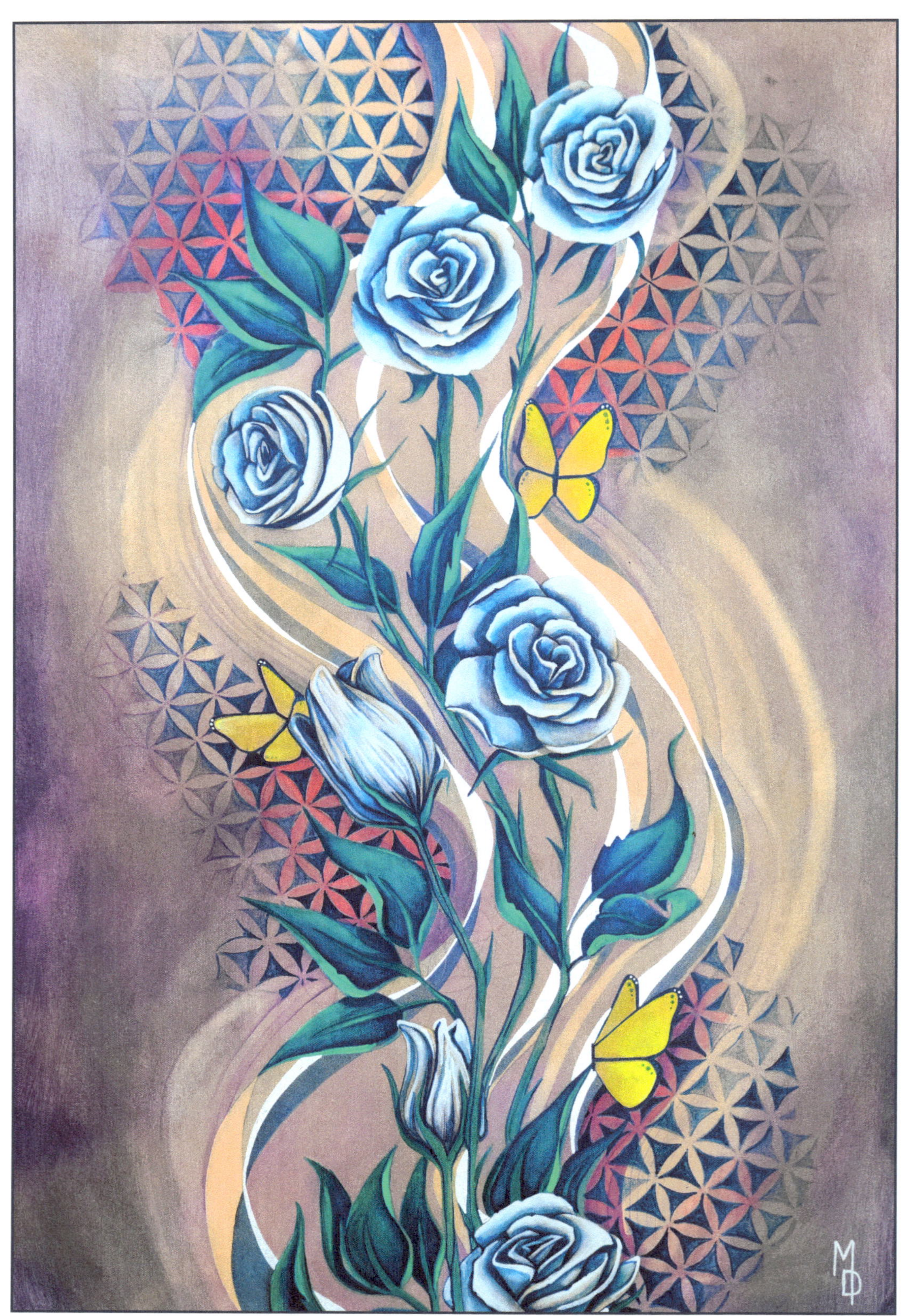

Sacred Blooms, 2024
24"x36"
Acrylic & Mixed Media on Canvas
Blacklight Enhanced

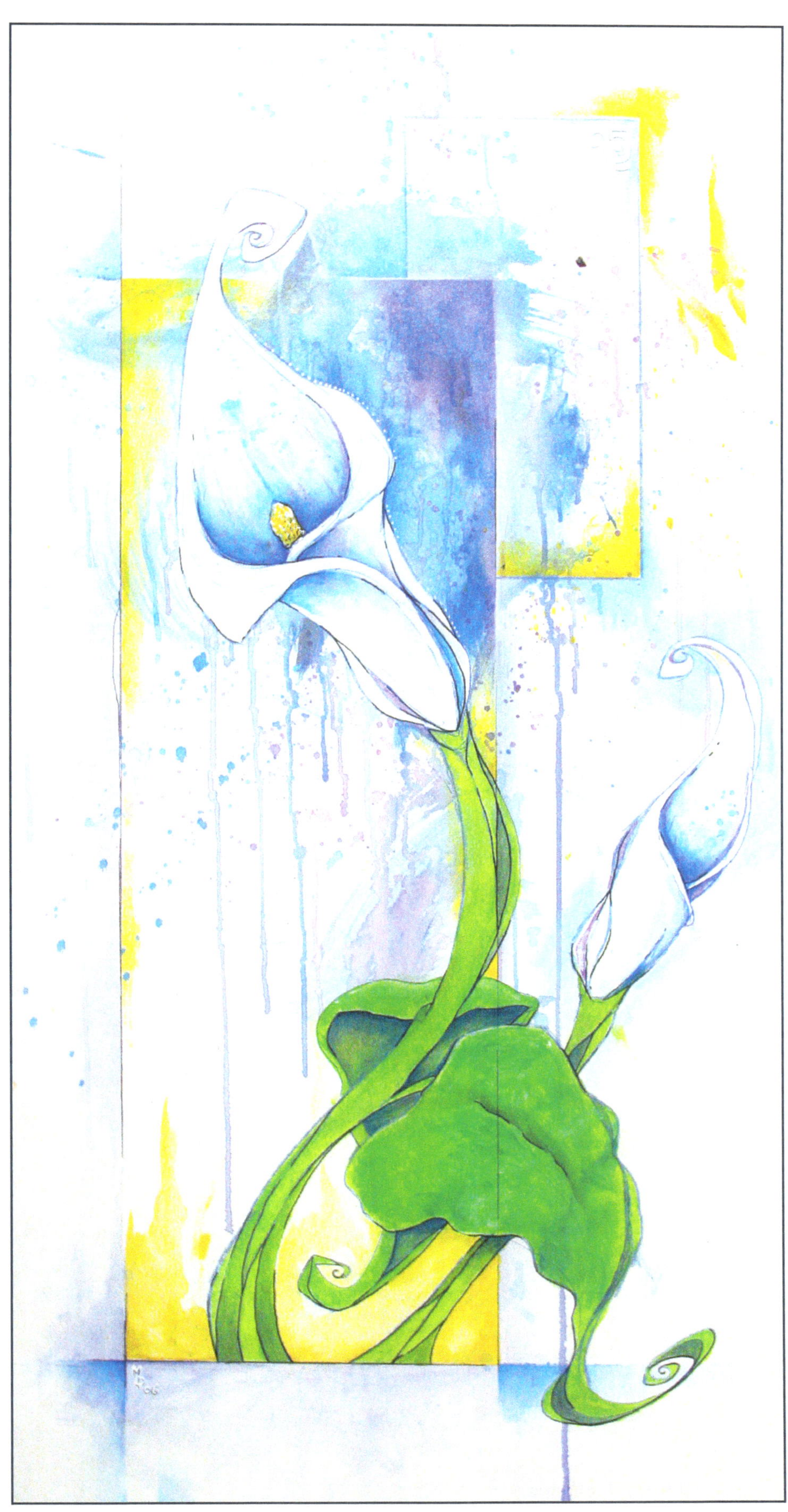

Calla Lilies and Squares,
2006
24"x48"
Acrylic & Mixed Media on Canvas

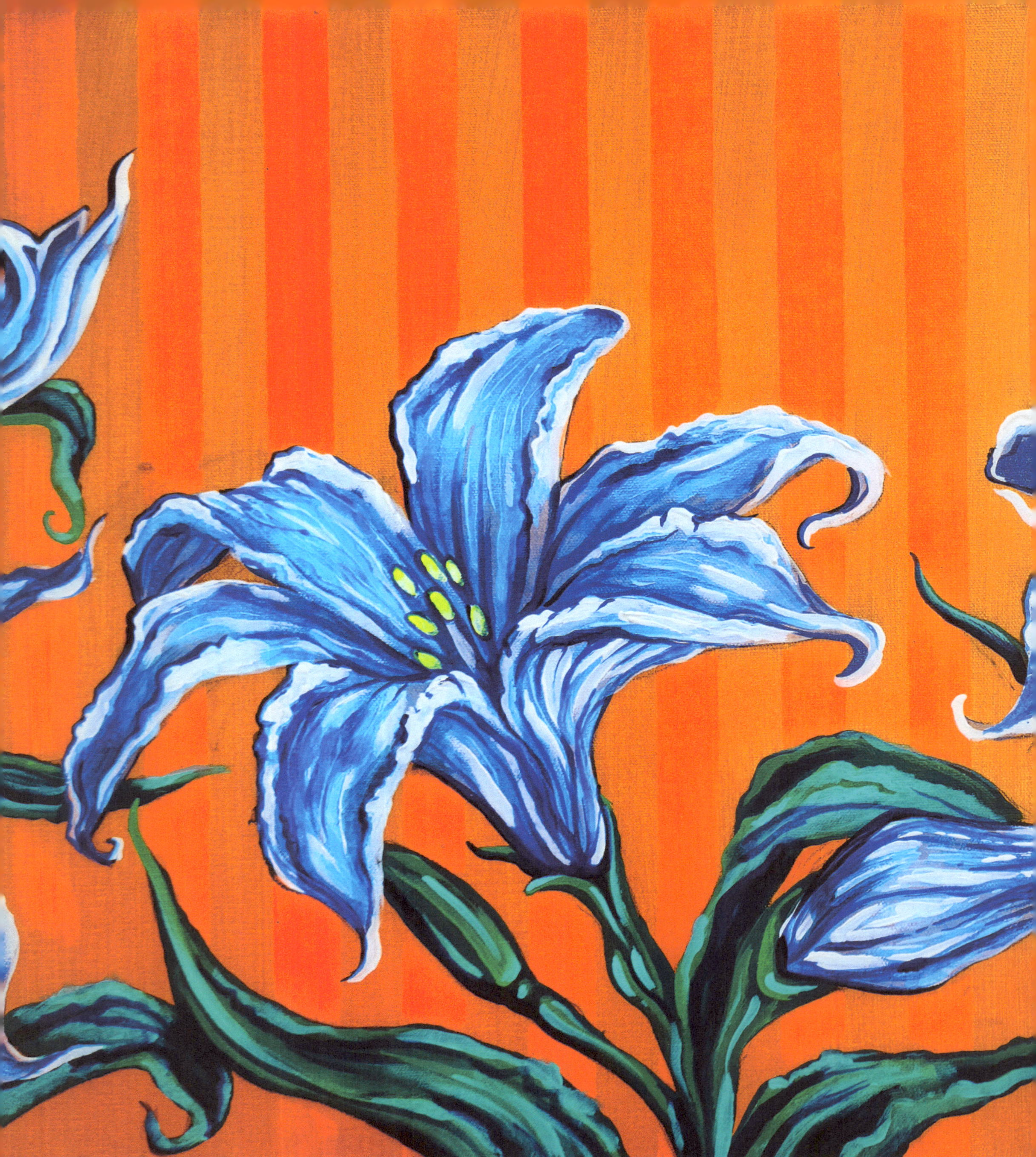

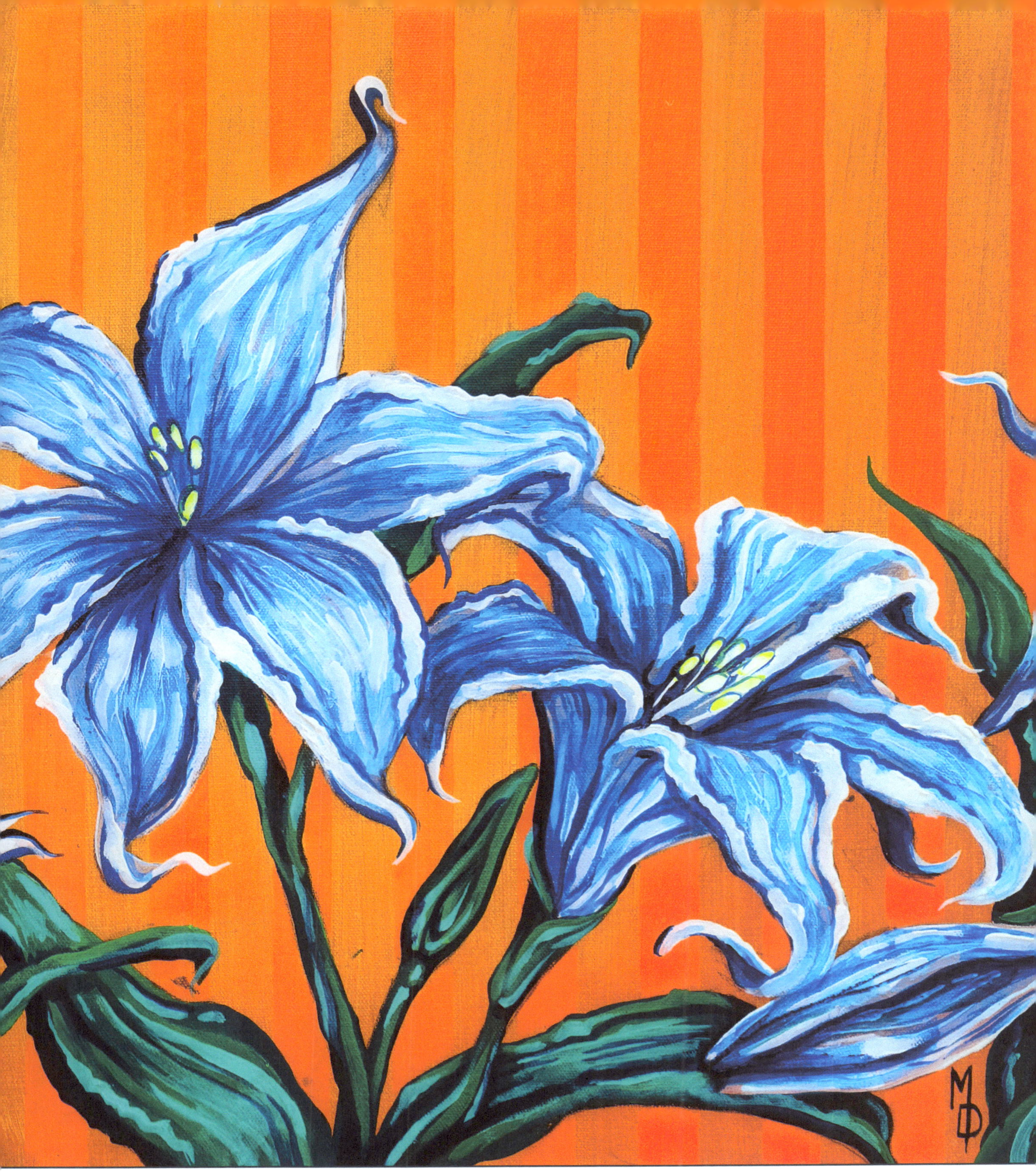

Blue Petals, 2022
36"x18"
Acrylic & Mixed Media on Canvas

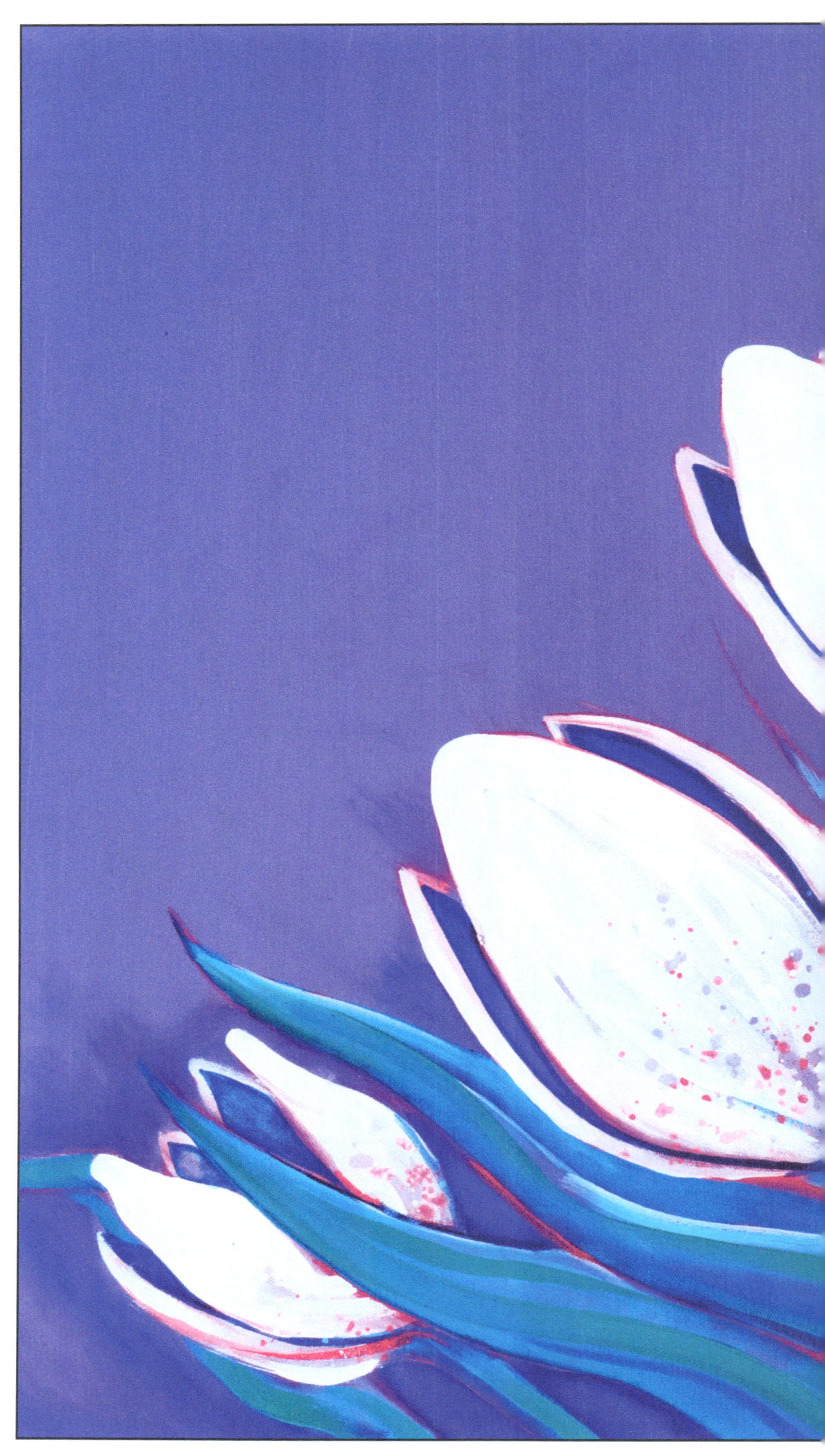

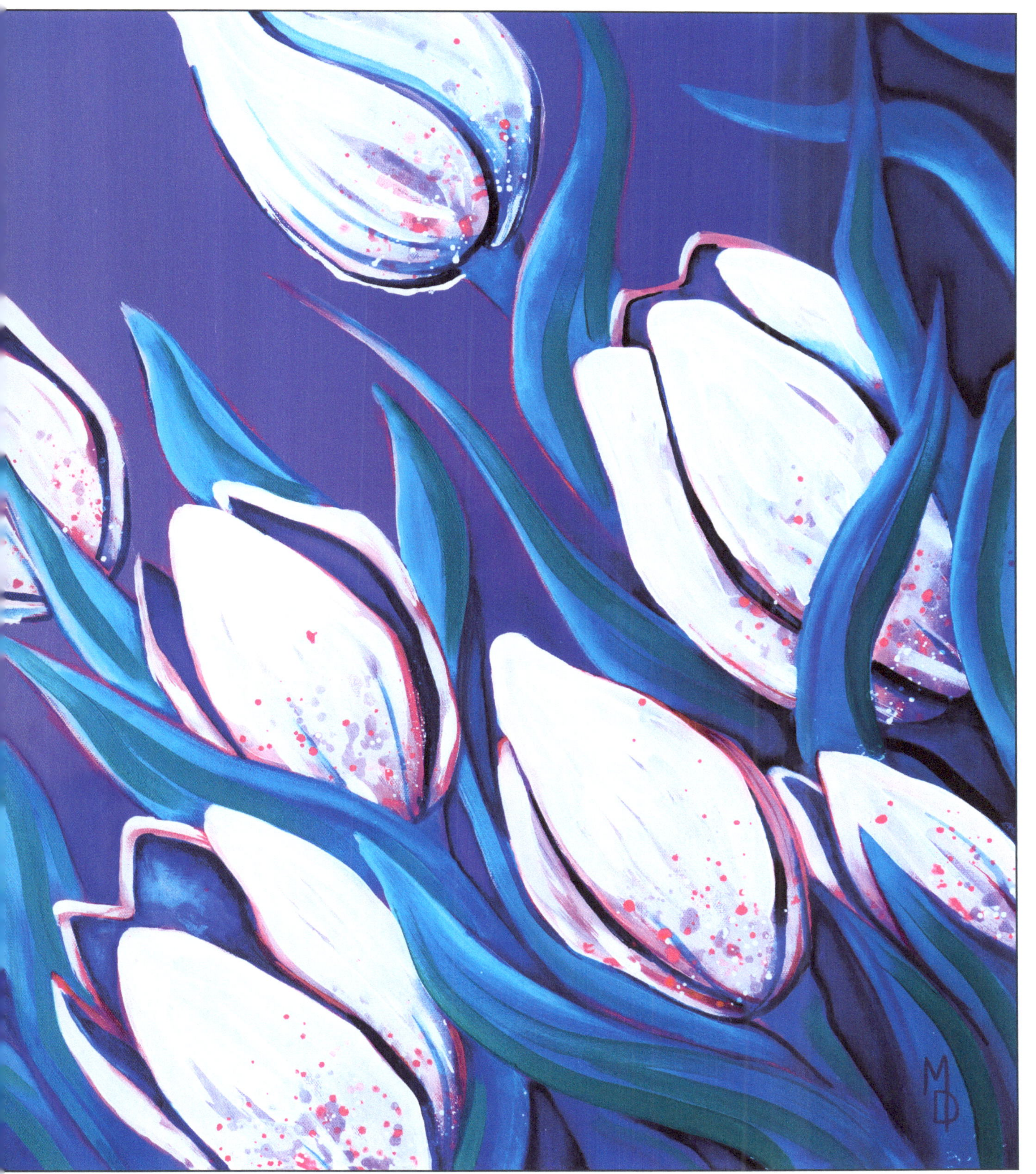

White Tulips on Lilac, 2024
36"x24"
Acrylic & Mixed Media on Canvas

Commissioned by a client who requested a wicked wildflower field, Miles filled the canvas with poisonous flowers including foxglove, poppies, and belladonna - deadly nightshade. The conceptual contrast of deadly beauty brings to focus the balance of life.

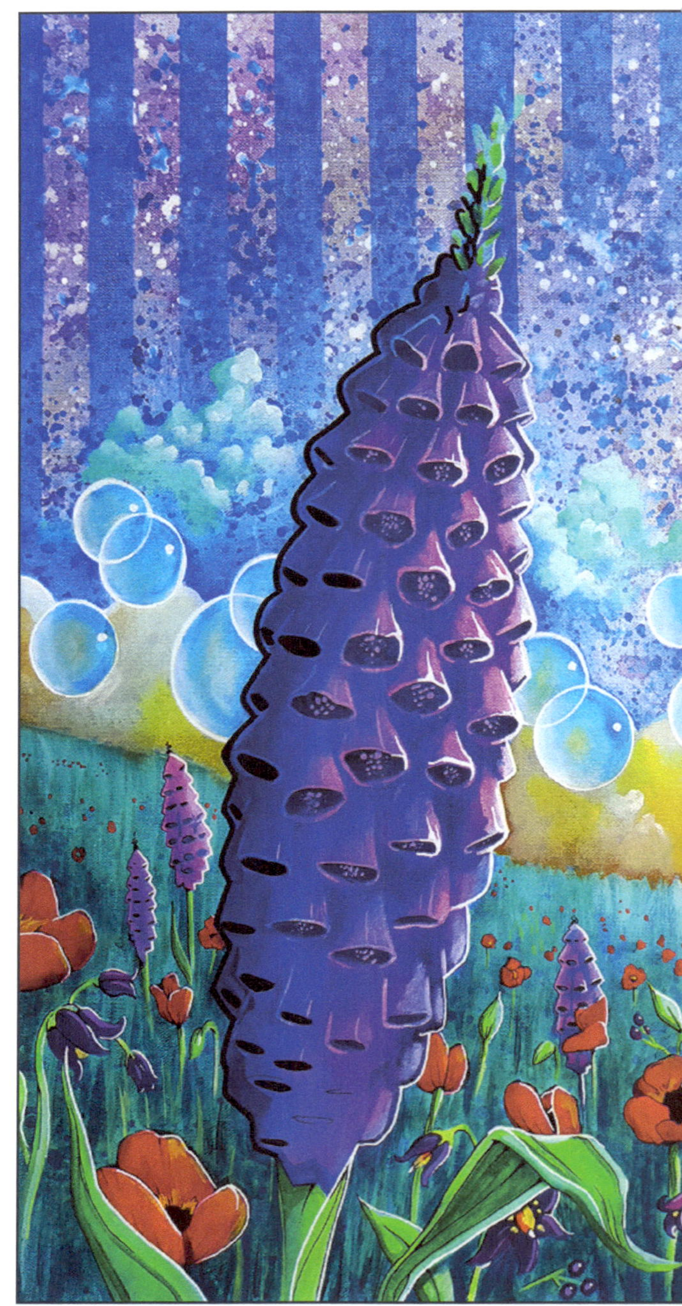

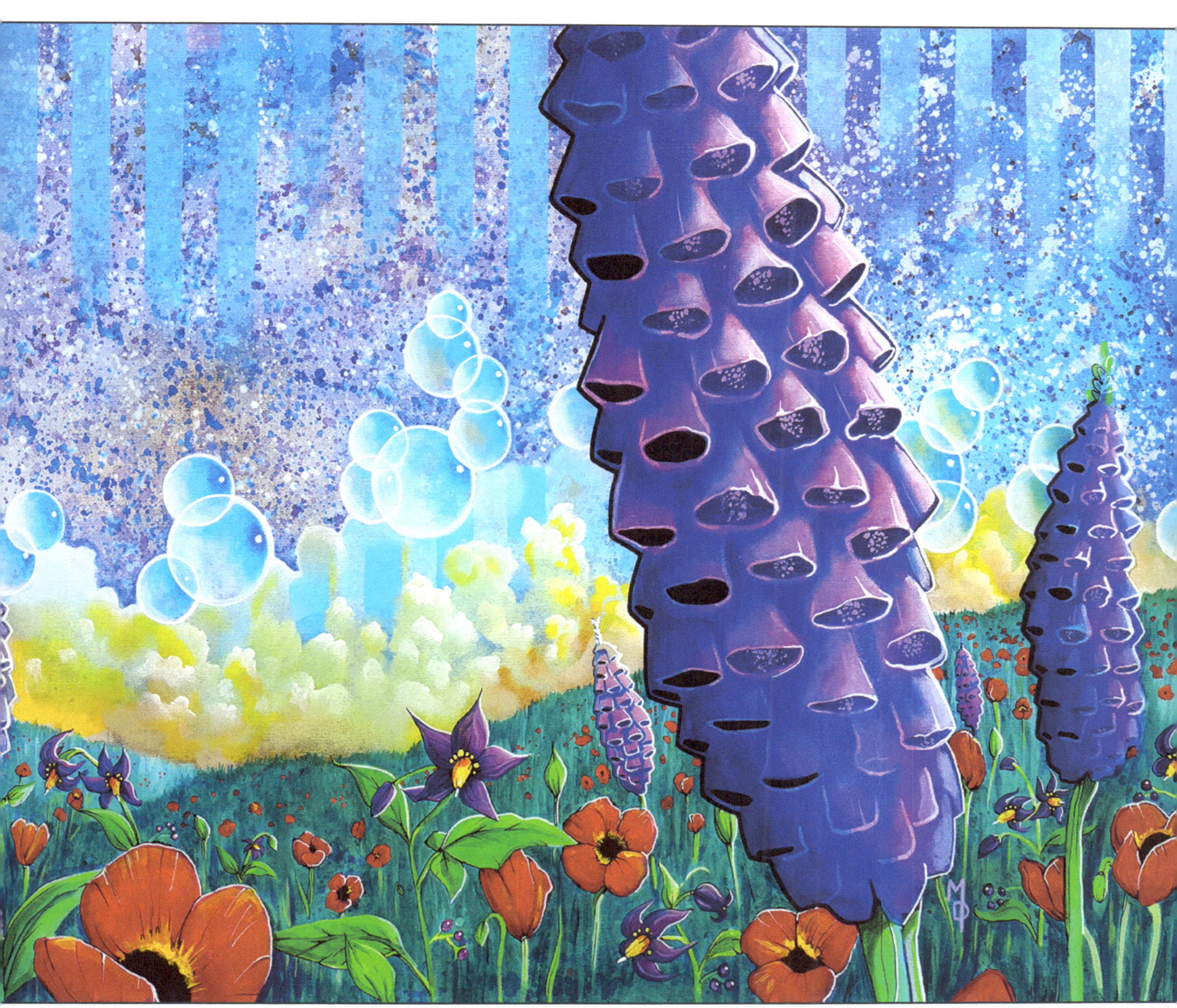

Deadly Garden, 2016
48"x24"
Acrylic & Mixed Media on Canvas

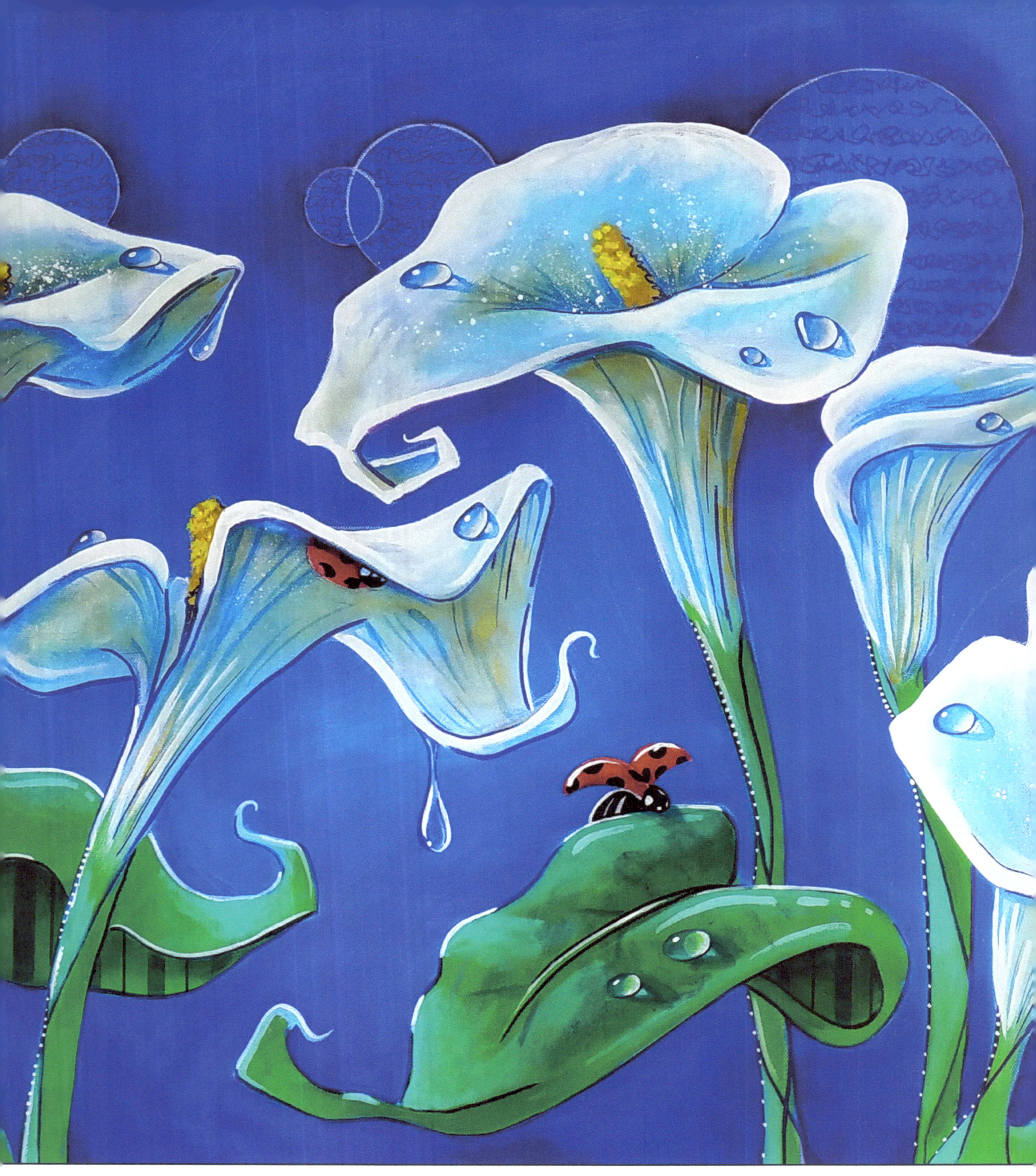

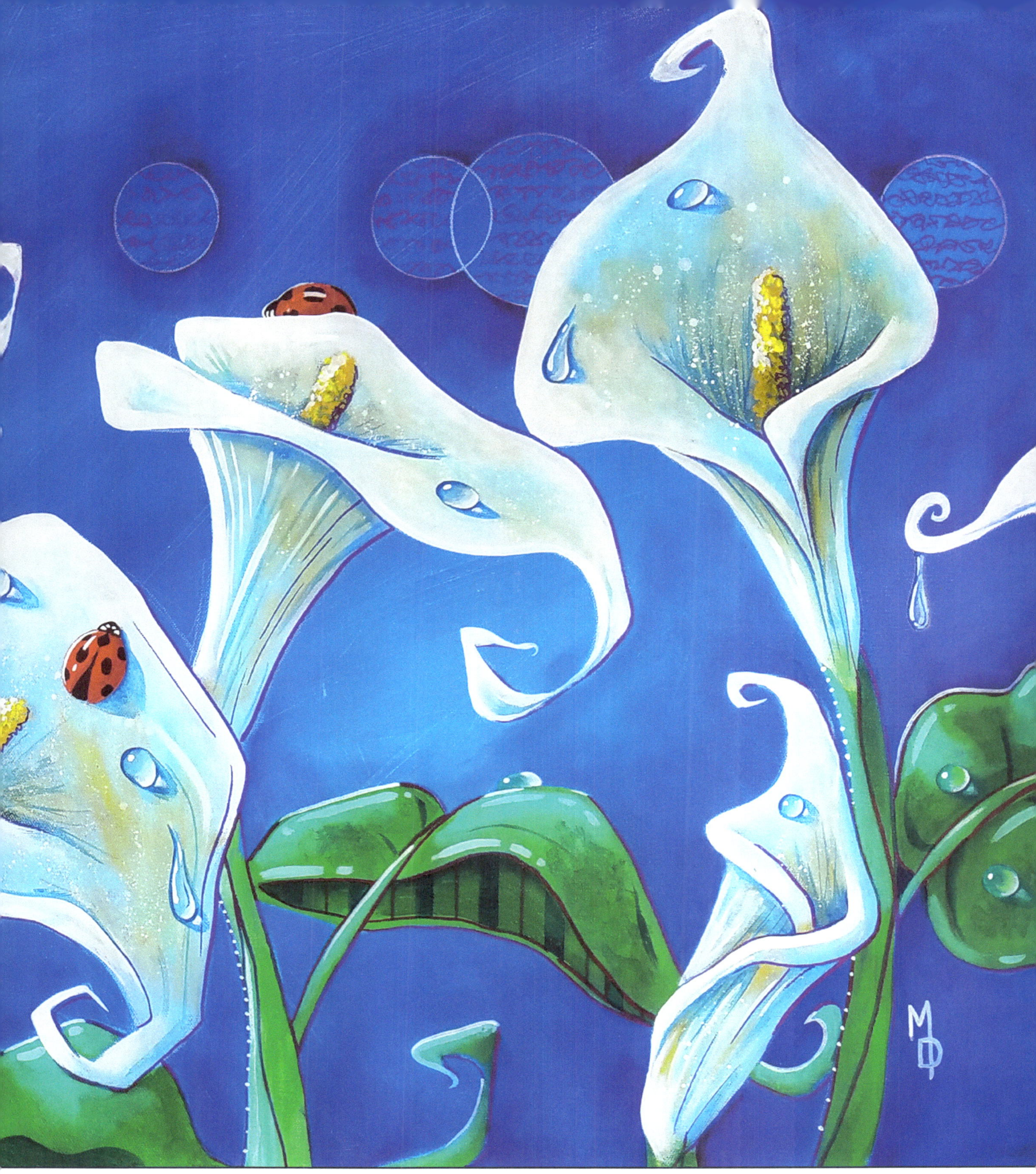

Calla Lilies for Lisa, 2018
48"x24"
Acrylic & Mixed Media on Canvas

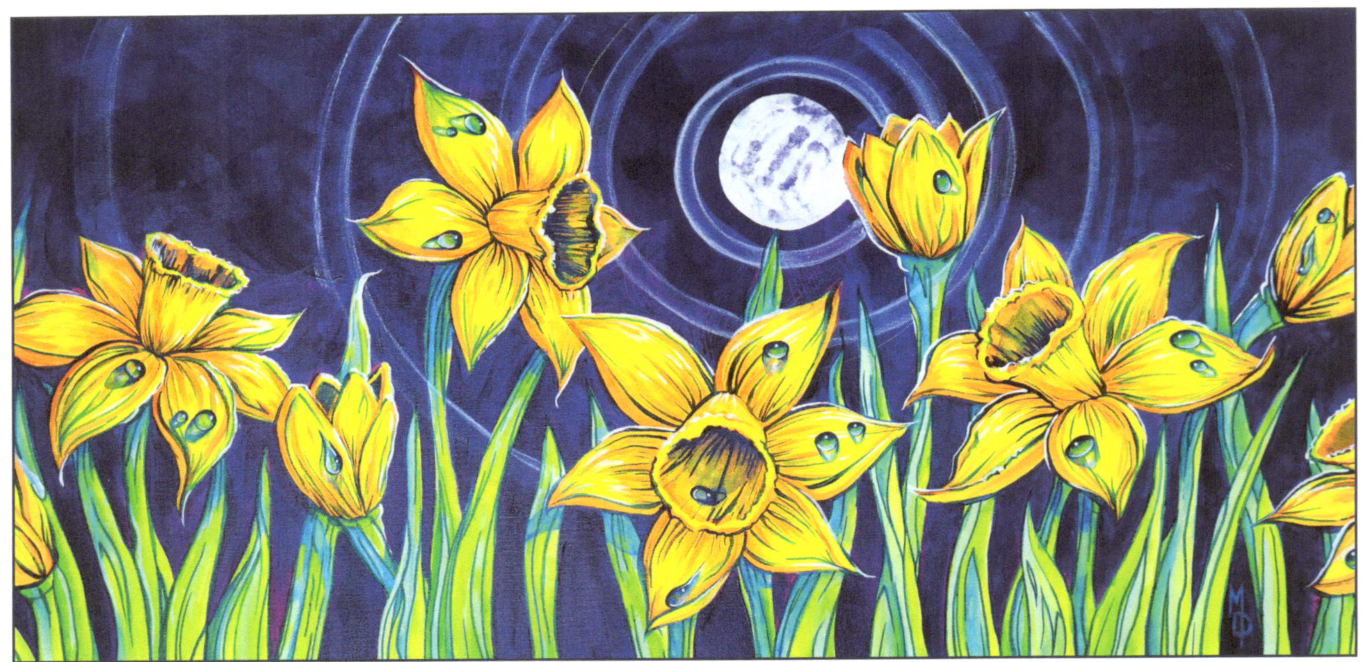

Drops of Jupiter, 2022
36"x18"
Acrylic & Mixed Media on Canvas

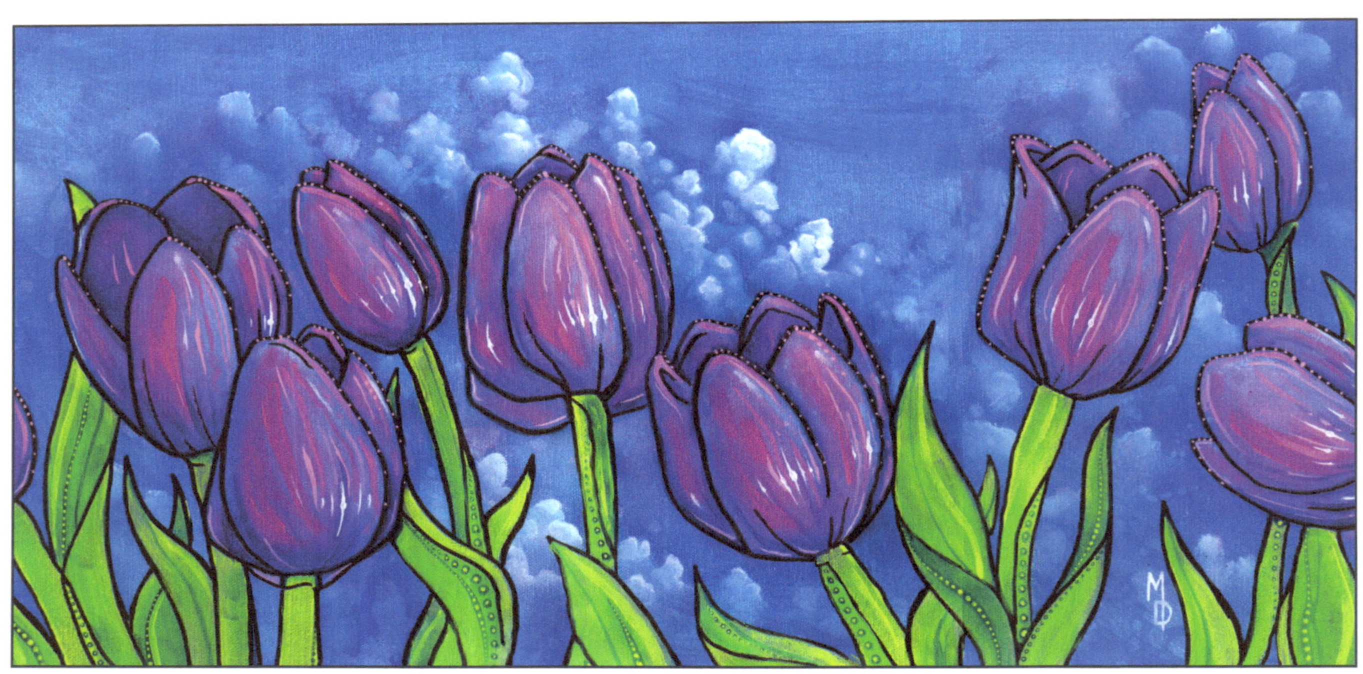

Tulips on Blue, 2014
24"x12"
Acrylic & Mixed Media on Canvas

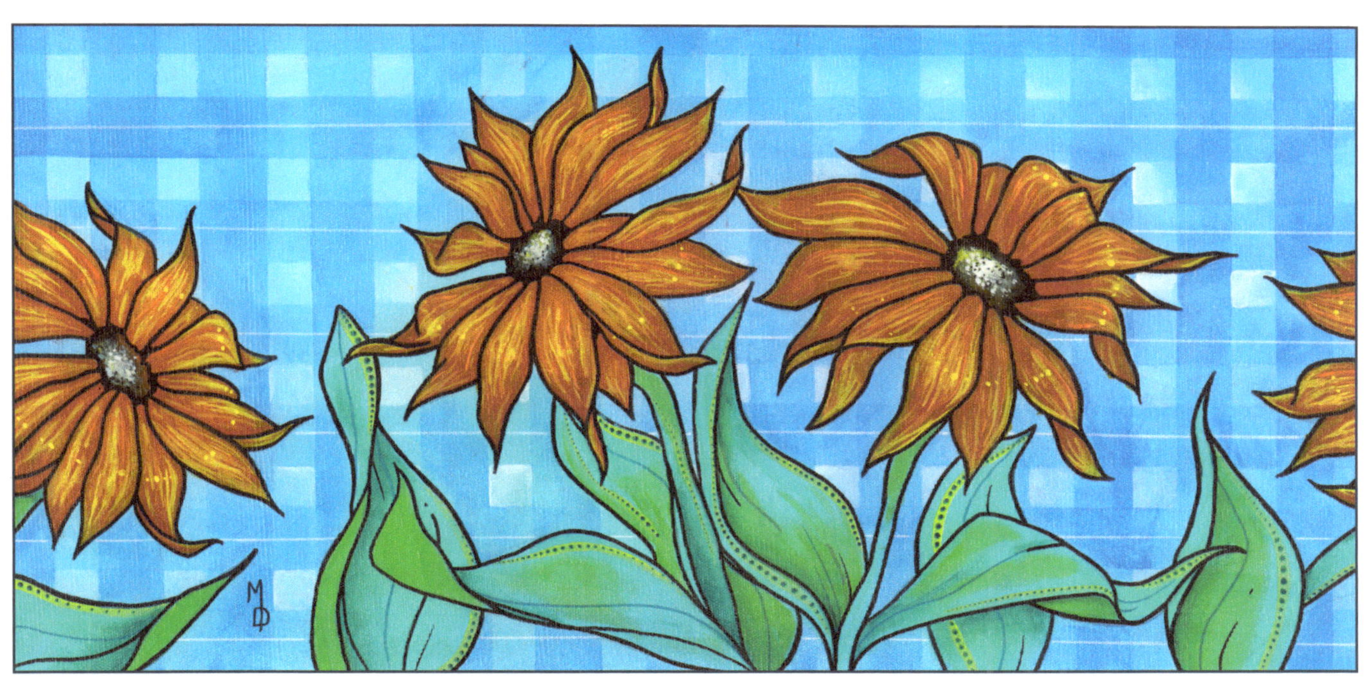

Susans in Plaid, 2016
24"x12"
Acrylic & Mixed Media on Canvas

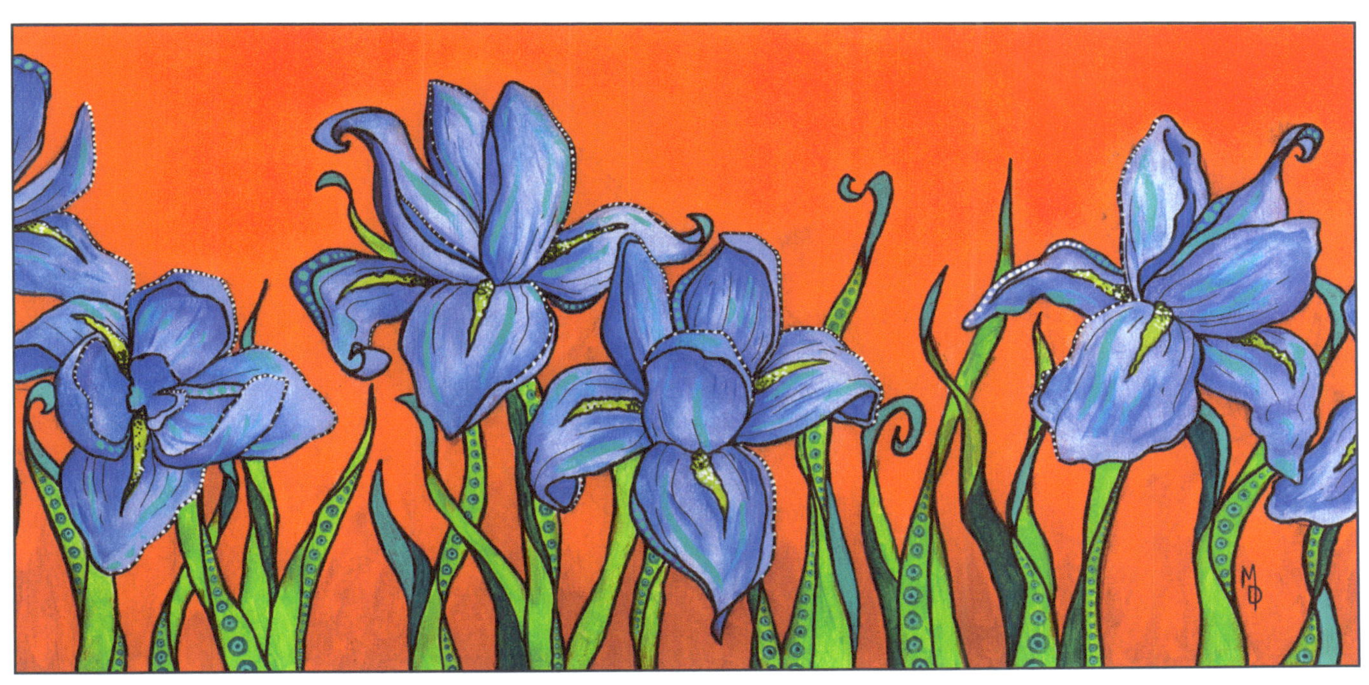

Blue Irises, 2014
24"x12"
Acrylic & Mixed Media on Canvas

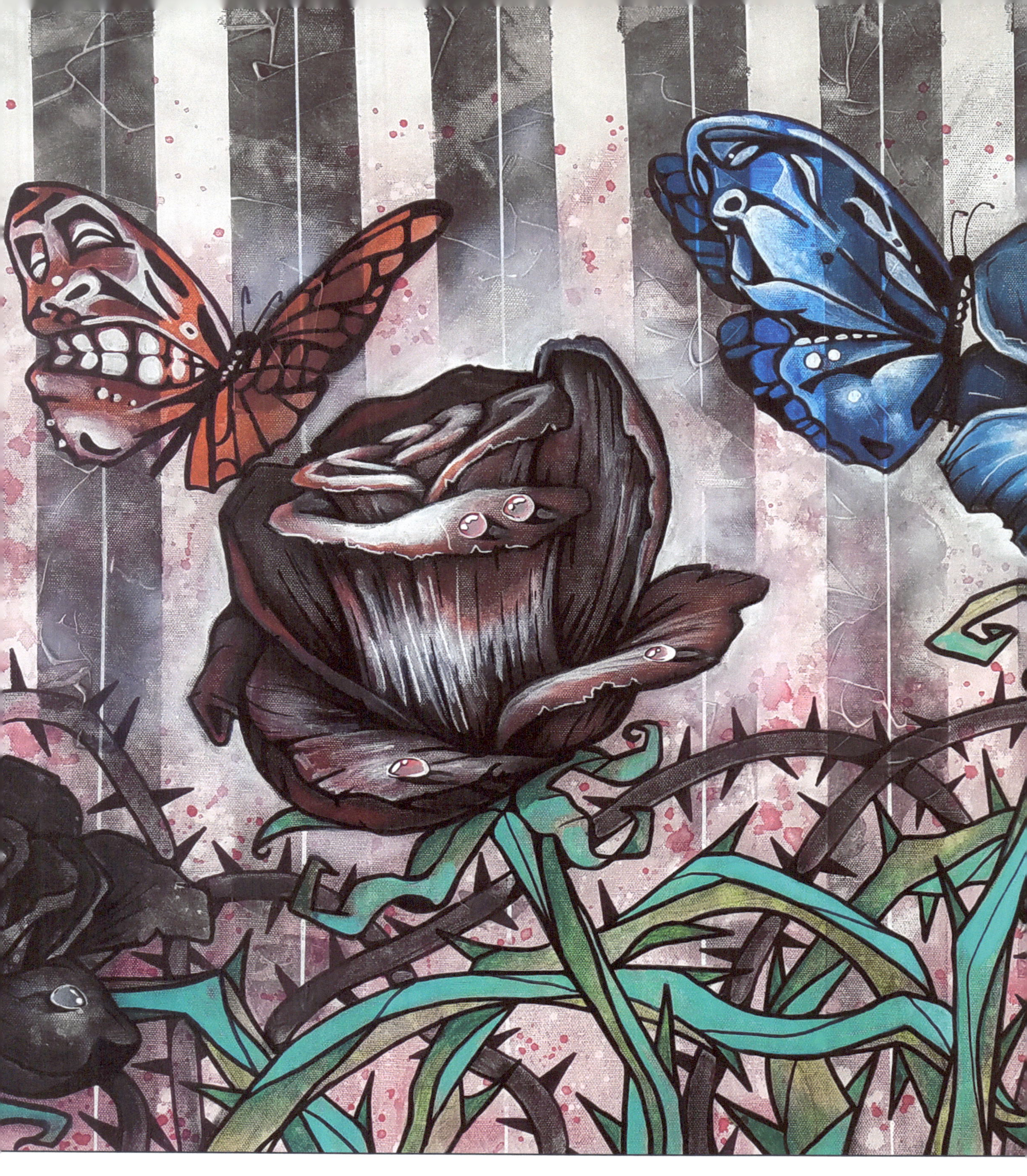

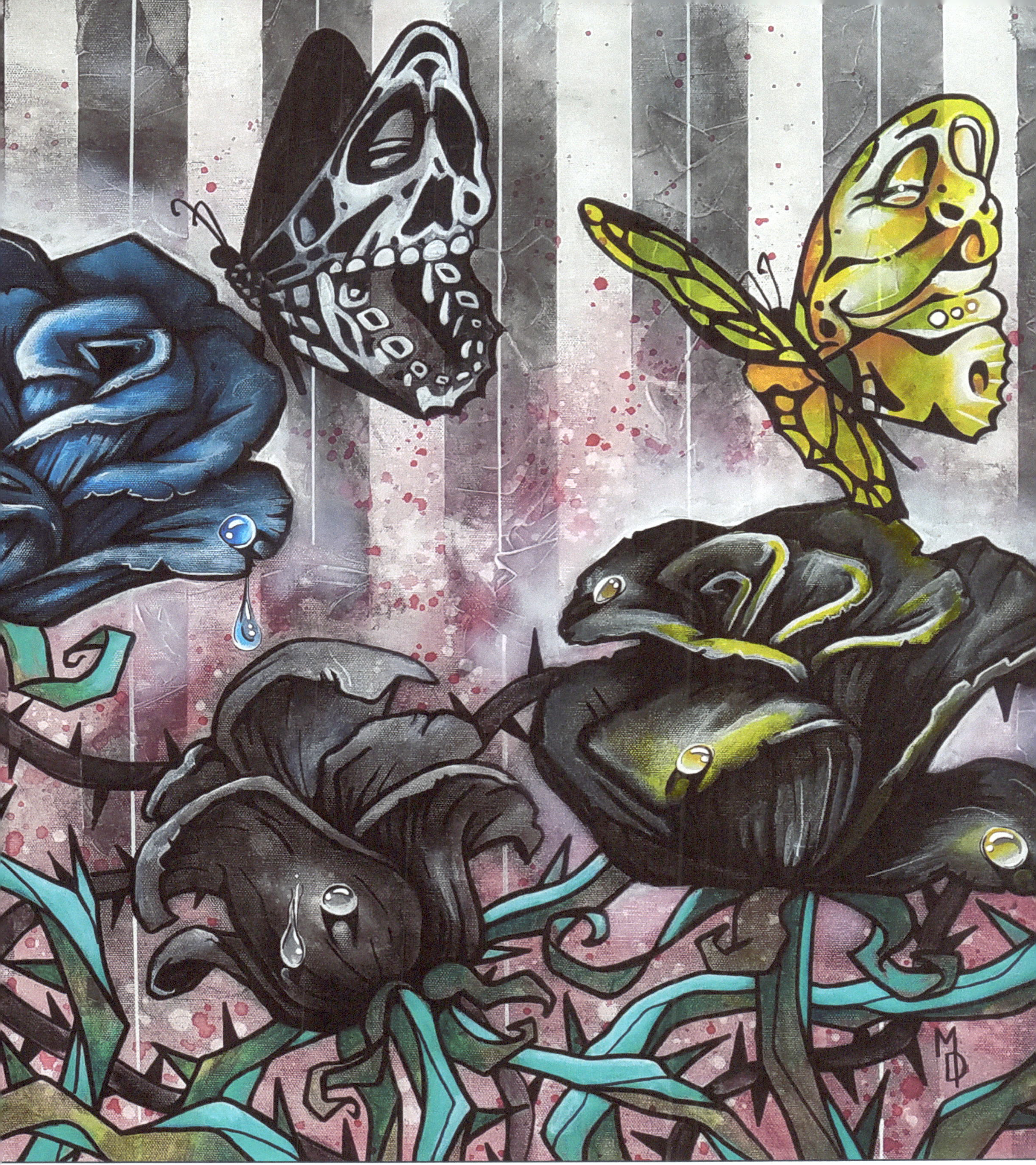

The Ghosts in the Garden, 2018
48"x24"
Acrylic & Mixed Media on Canvas

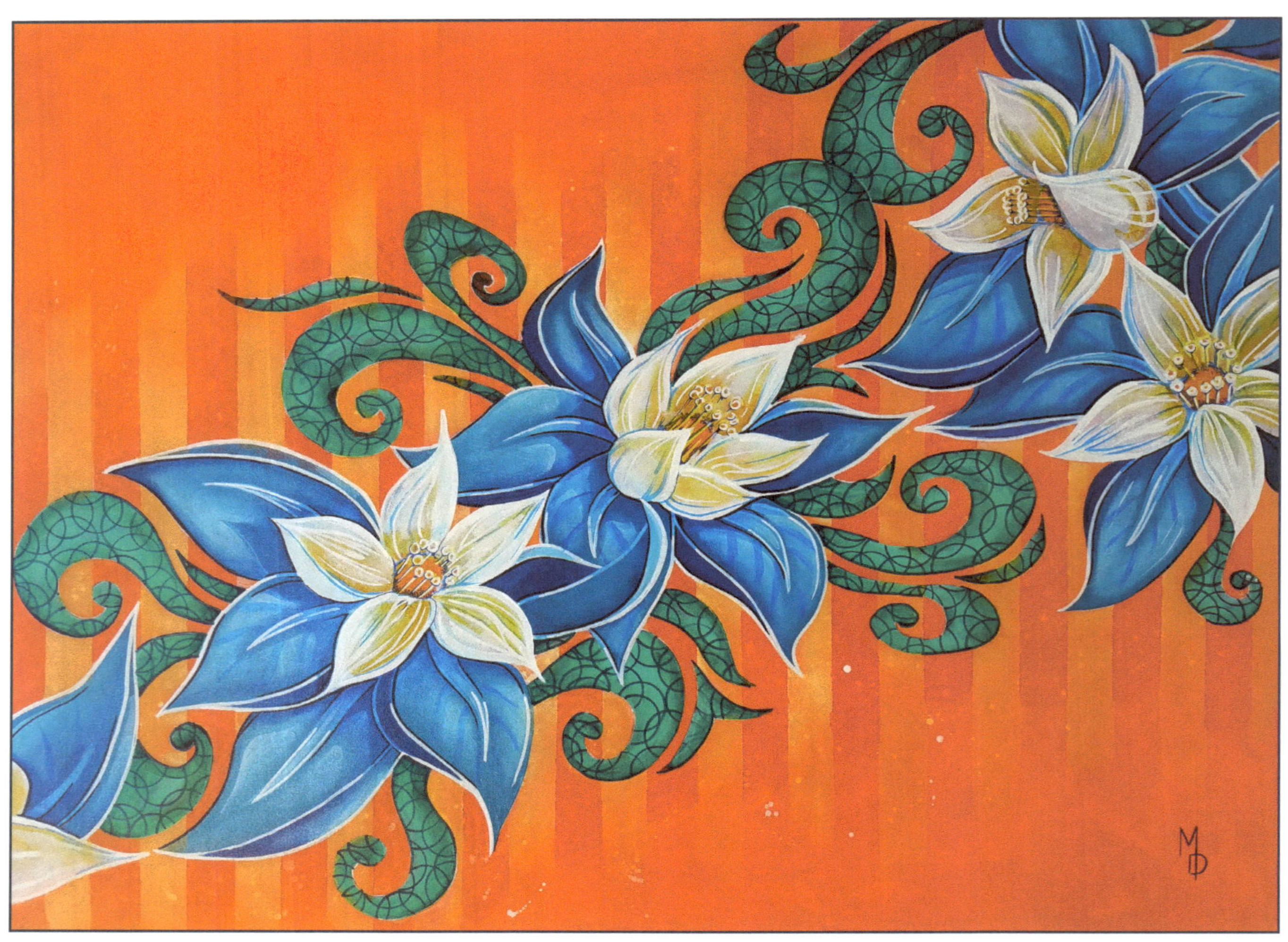

Clementine Flowers, 2017
40"x30"
Acrylic & Mixed Media on Canvas

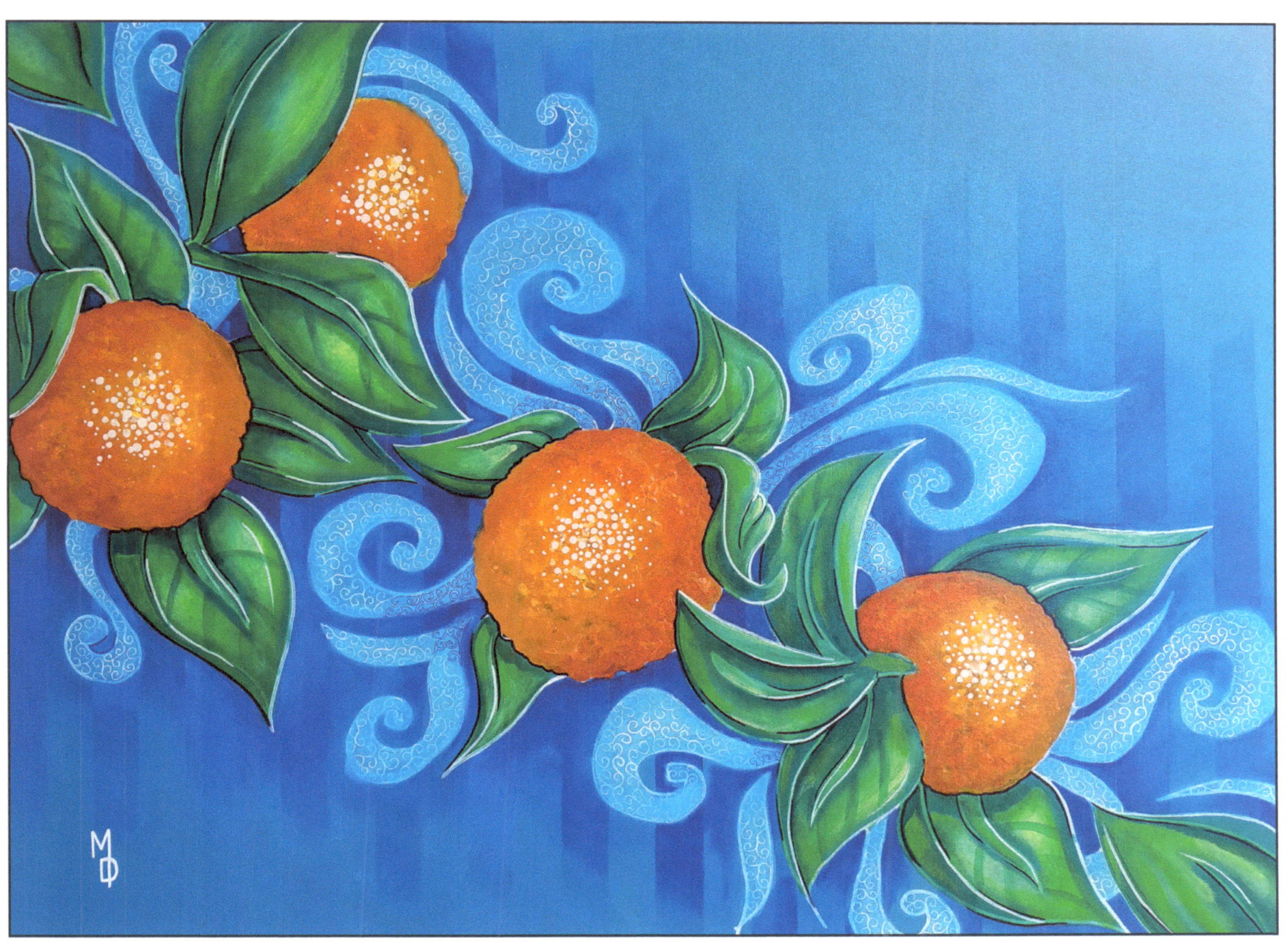

Clementine Fruit, 2017
40"x30"
Acrylic & Mixed Media on Canvas

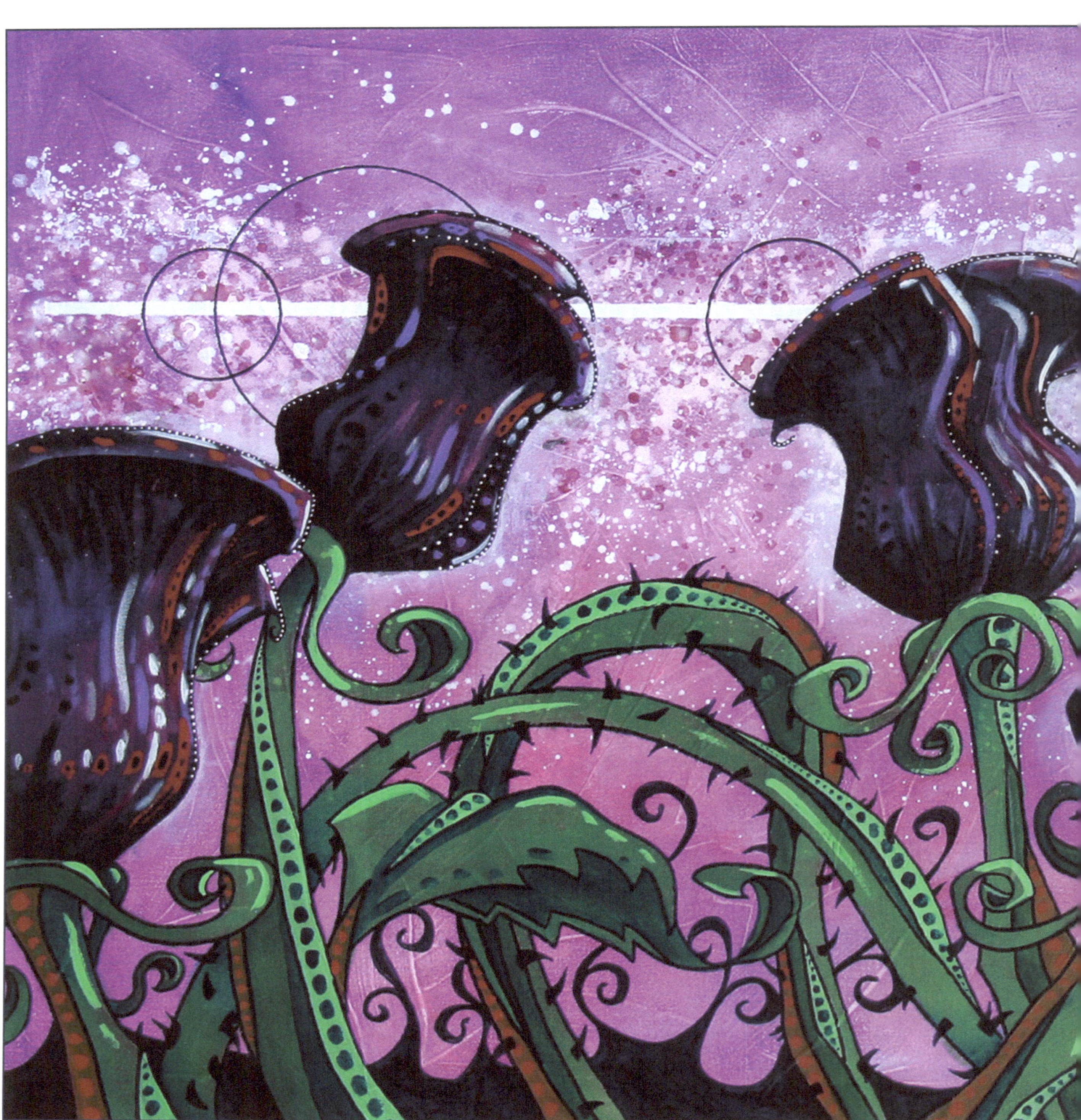

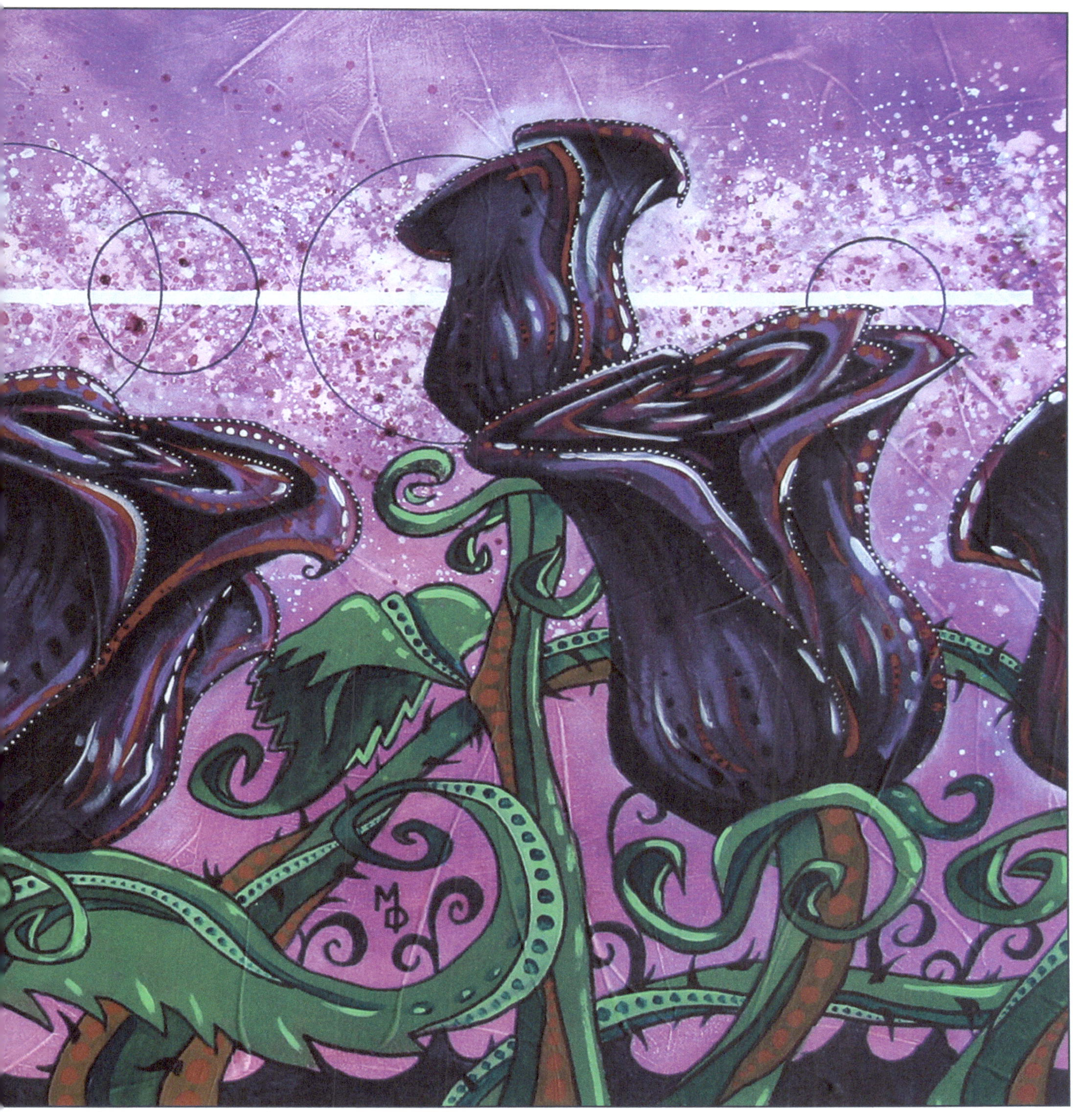

Black Roses #2, 2009
48"x24"
Acrylic & Mixed Media on Canvas

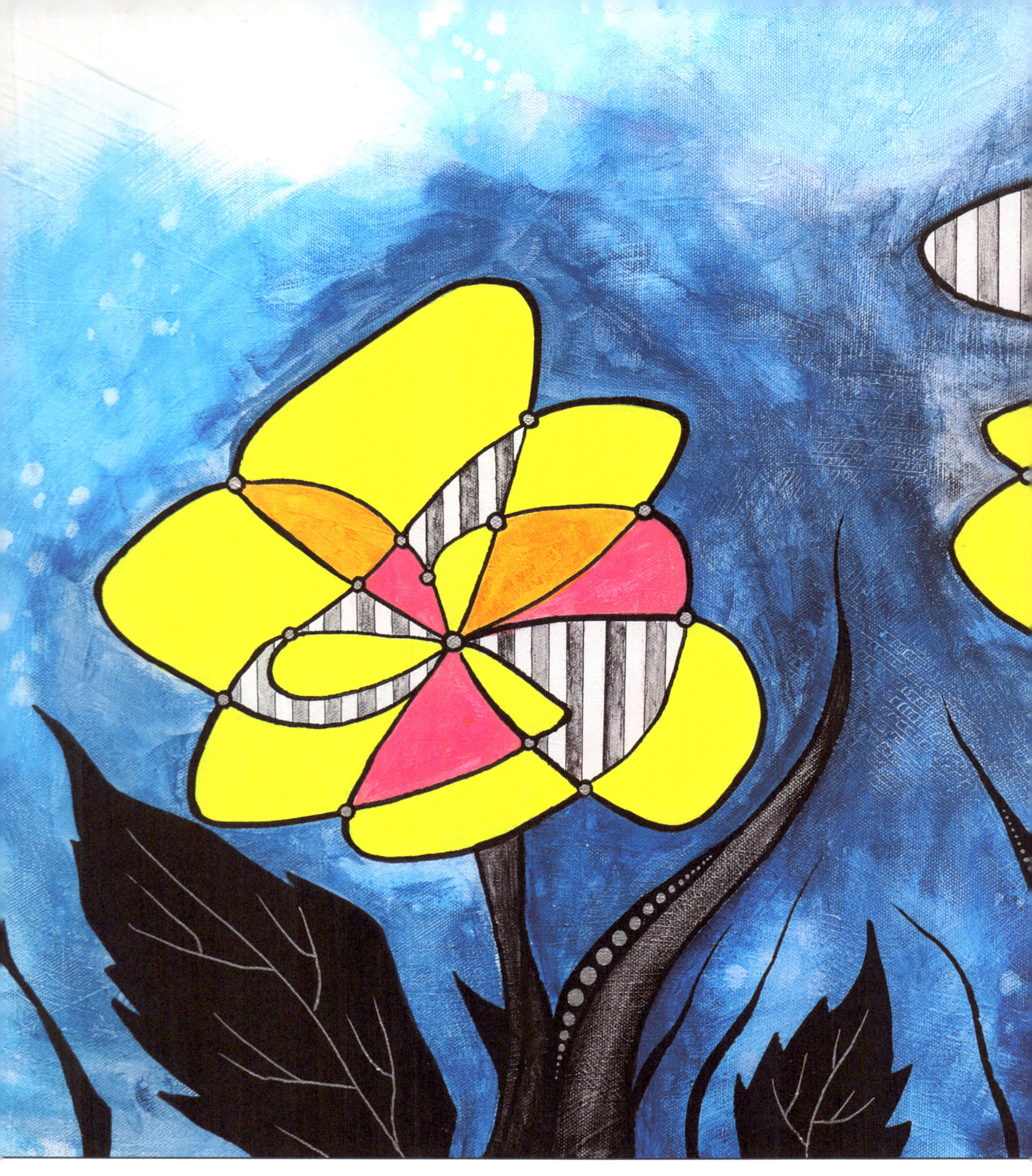

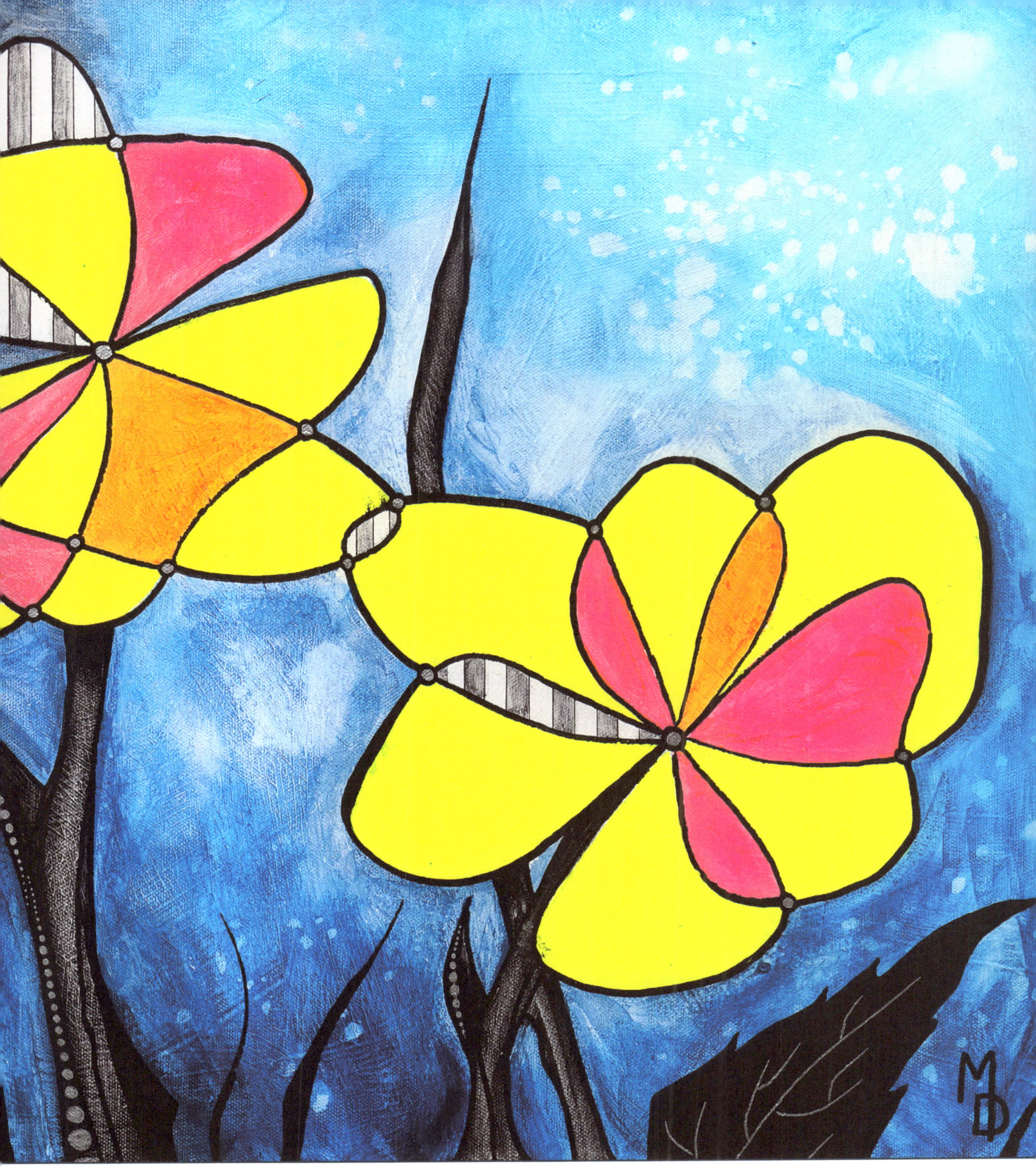

Atomic Blooms, 2023
36"x18"
Acrylic & Mixed Media on Canvas
Blacklight Enhanced

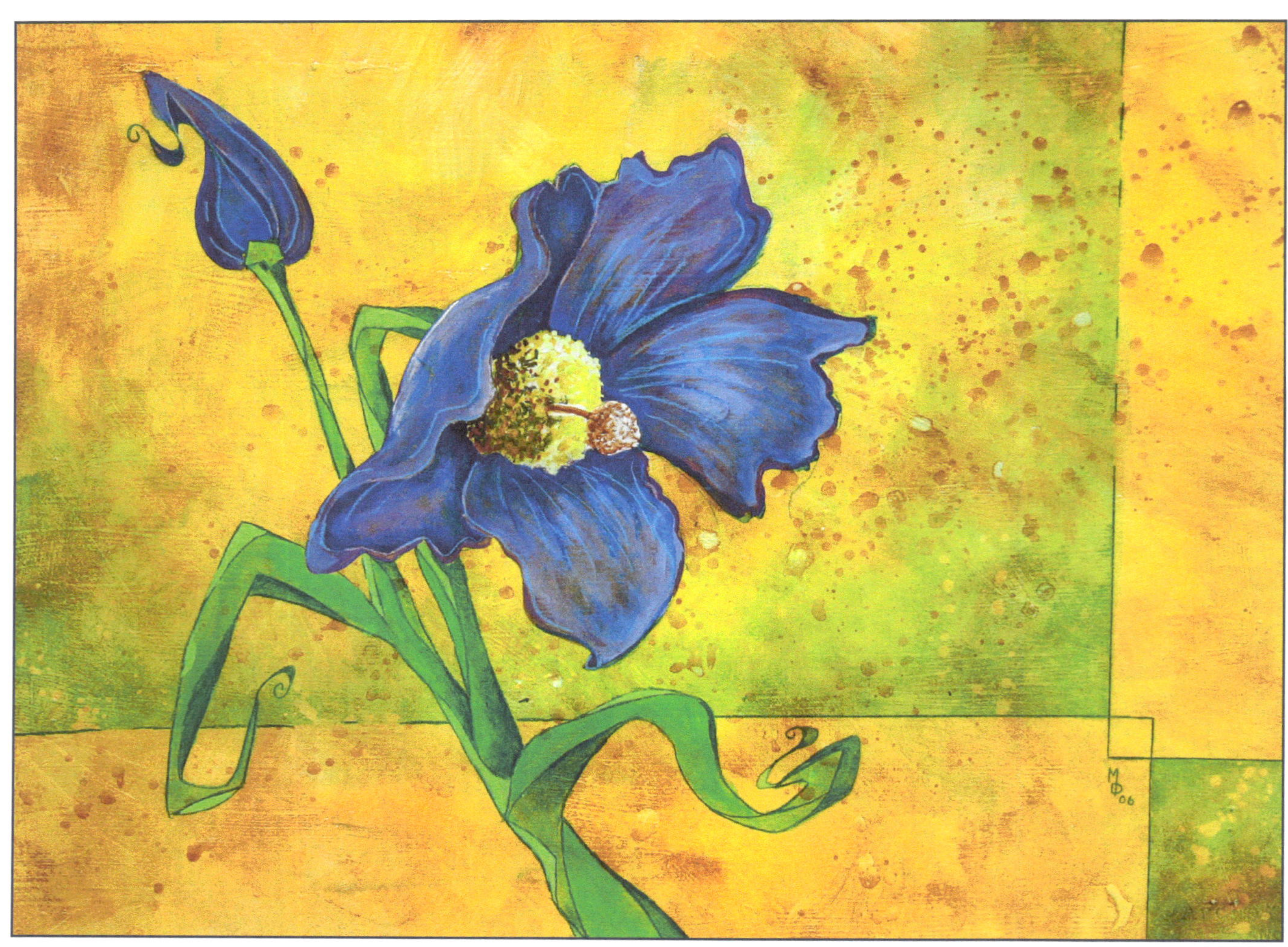

Blue Poppy #1, 2006
29"x21"
Acrylic & Mixed Media on Paper

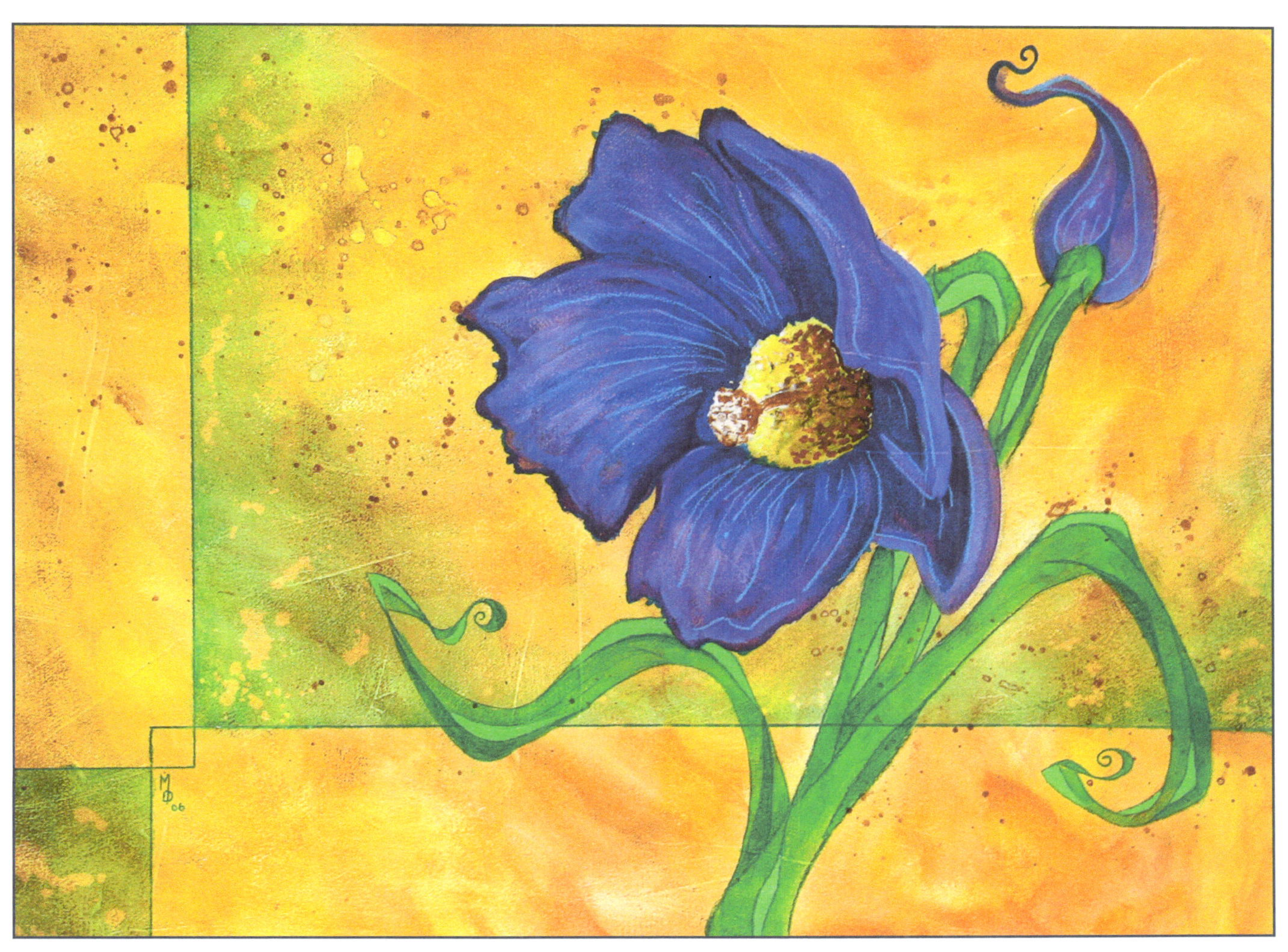

Blue Poppy #2, 2006
29"x21"
Acrylic & Mixed Media on Paper

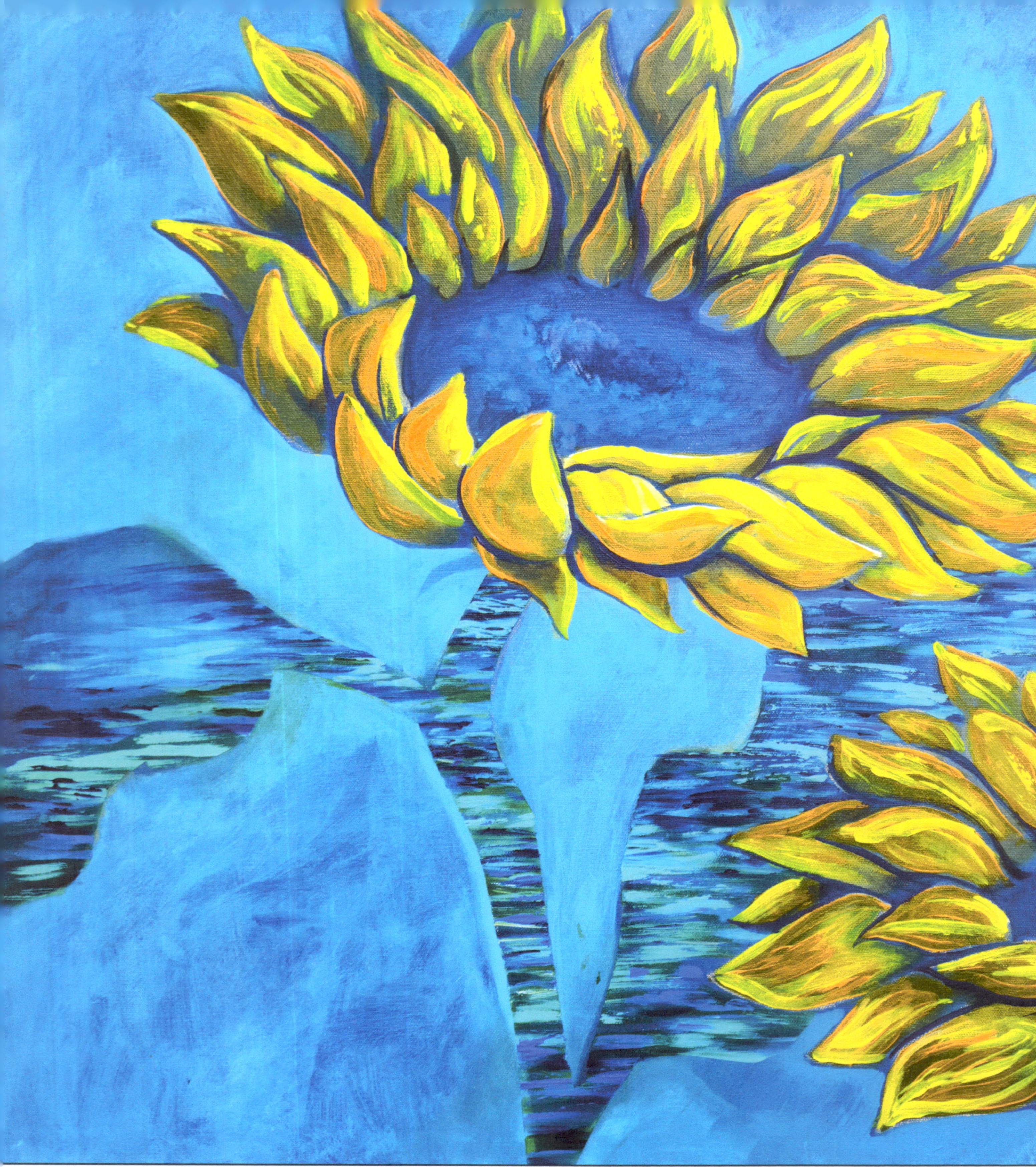

Sunflowers and Static #1, 2024
36"x24"
Acrylic & Mixed Media on Canvas

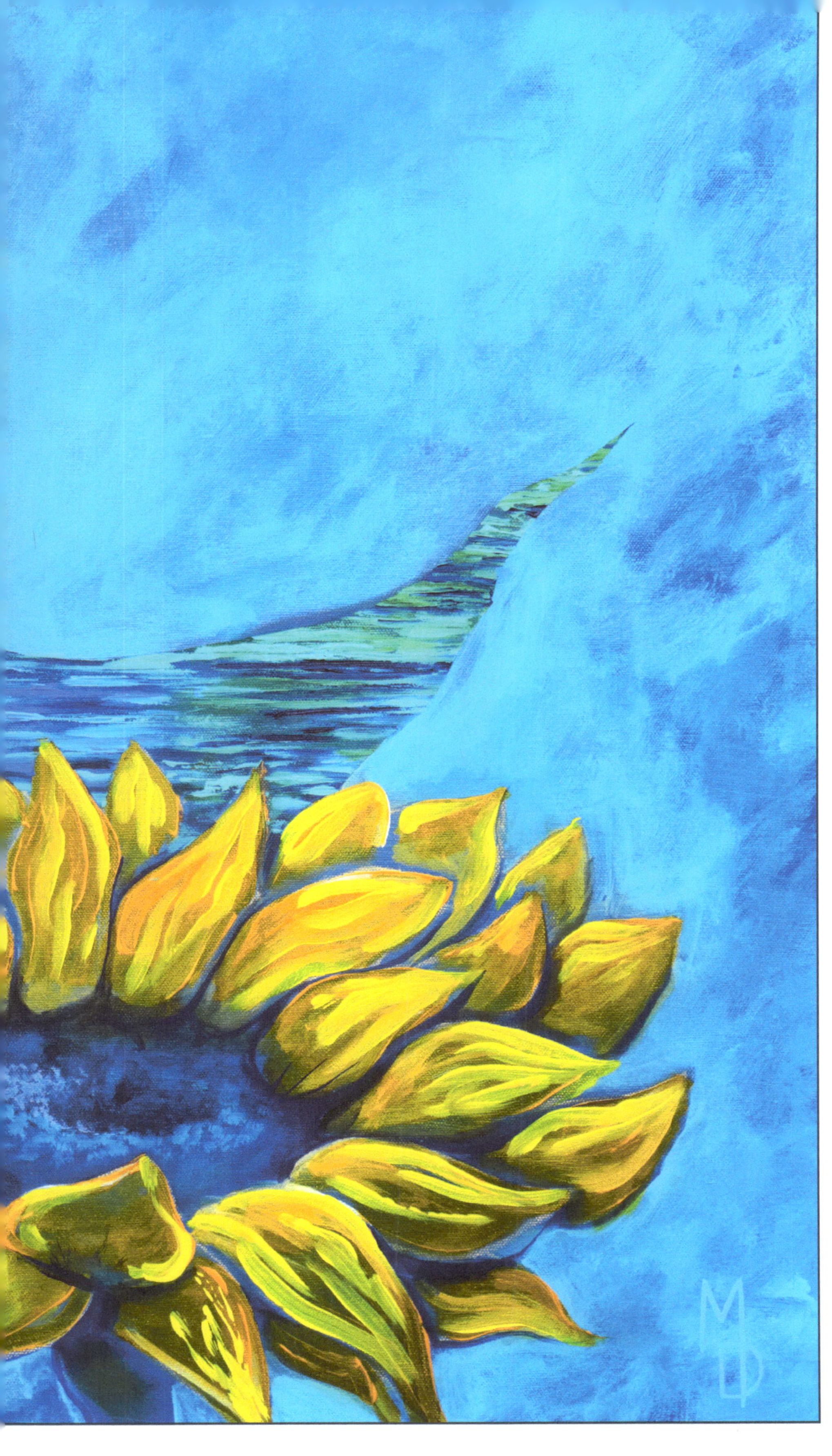

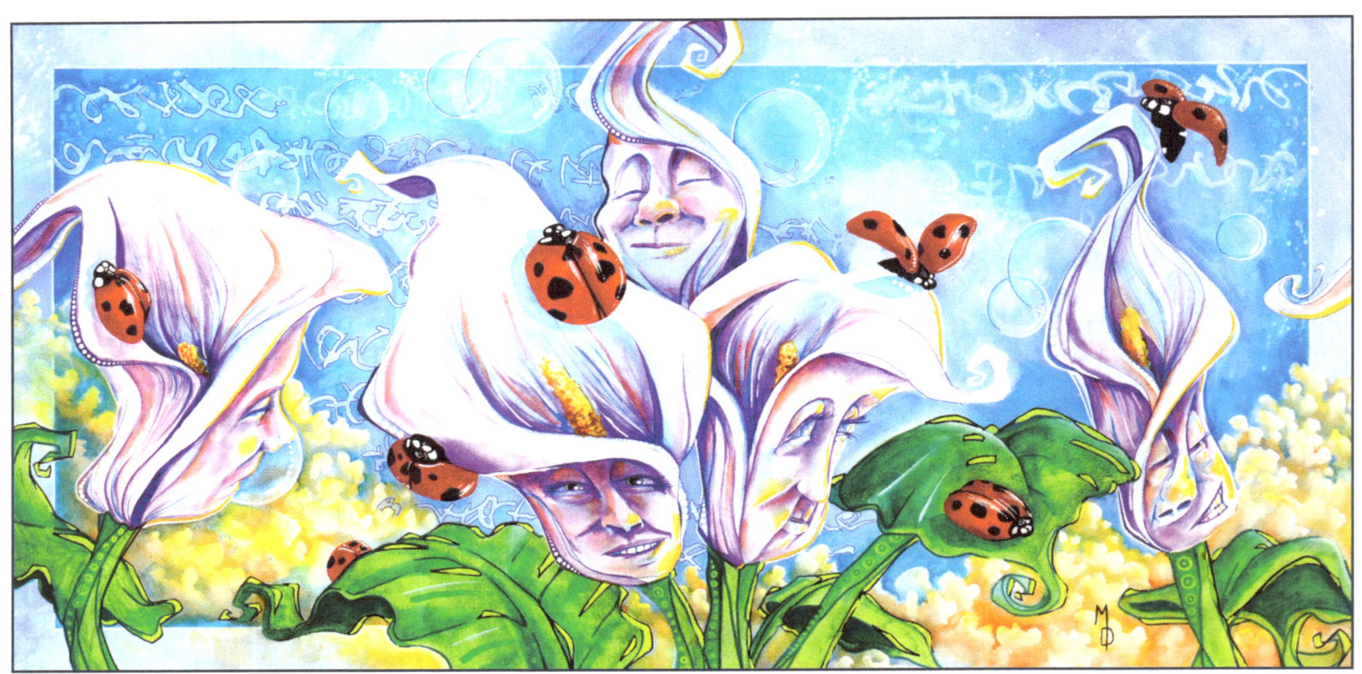

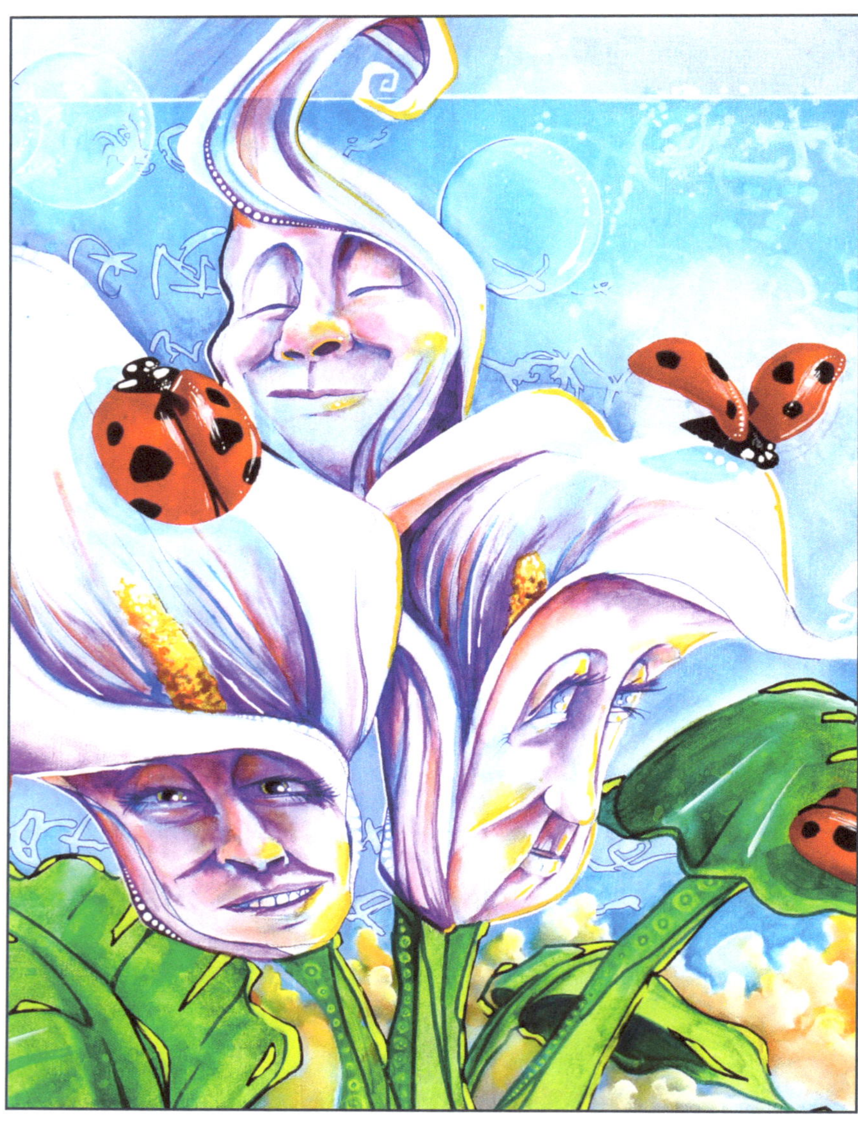

Rockalilies, 2015
48"x24"
Acrylic & Mixed Media on Canvas

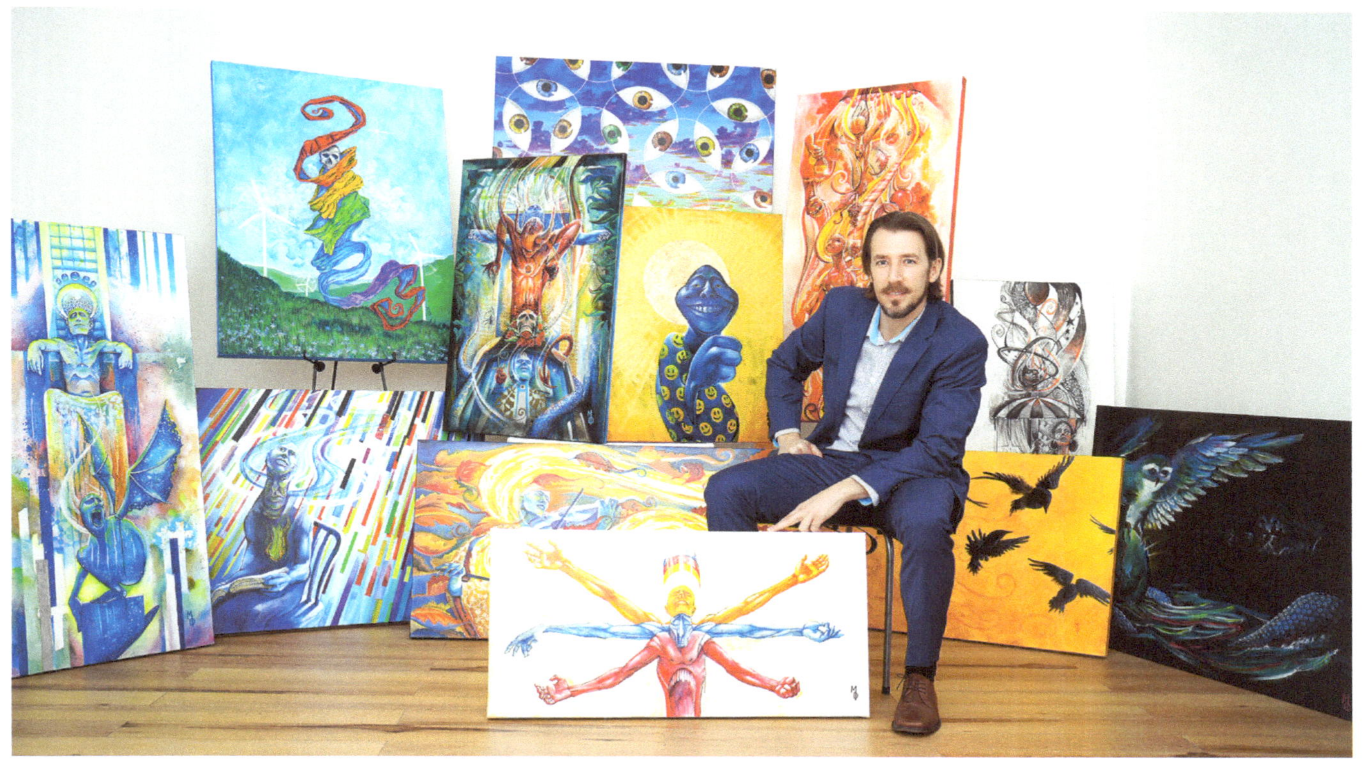

Miles Davis

Through painting, Miles explores the crossroads of modern spirituality and science and seeks to examine those complexities in an honest way. Inspired by the evolving relationship between personal and cultural identity, he uses crisp illustrative aesthetics and dramatic symbolism to engage the viewer. Striving for a unique accessibility, Miles endeavors to bypass perceived elitist tendencies and create work that speaks to everyone despite their art education.

Since 2003, Miles has been building his art practice through personal work, commissions, and public art. He has been included in grant projects from the National Endowment for the Arts and has received numerous awards for his paintings. Miles exhibits both nationally and internationally and made his debut solo museum exhibition in 2022 with "Vibrant Shadows" at the Marietta Cobb Museum of Art. For more information on Miles and his work, explore the other books in the Studio Collections series and visit massiveburn.com.

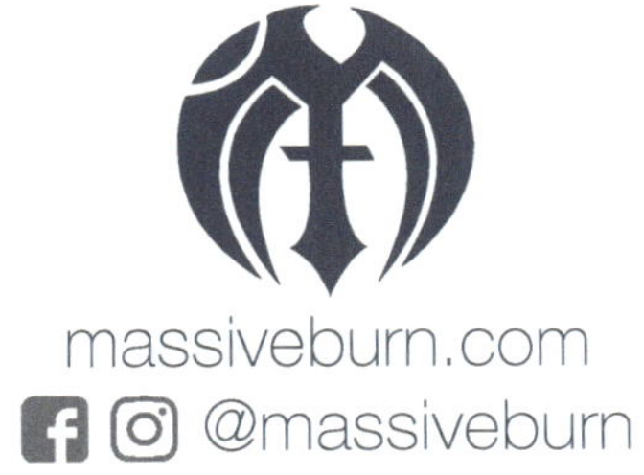

massiveburn.com

@massiveburn

www.ingramcontent.com/pod-product-compliance
Lightning Source LLC
LaVergne TN
LVHW070153110826
845147LV00002B/387
9798991881623